WHAT PEOPLE
"TWO NICKELS AND A DIME"

"Two Nickels And a Dime is an absolute must read for everyone. It is a truly rewarding story that leaves the reader wishing that it would never end."-

JOHNNIE MINICK, ENTERTAINER/RECORDING ARTIST

"This compelling story is beyond inspiring! No matter who you are, you never know the impact of a simple gesture."-

JENNIE FINCH, U.S. OLYMPIC GOLD MEDALIST

"This work of Lyndon Livingston's is not only a testimony but an excellent read. Much like Robert Morris's, 'Blessed Life', Lyndon has shared a message that will certainly edify the Body of Christ, and reveals both to believers and non-believers God's grace through supernatural giving."-

HUNTER LUNDY, AUTHOR/ATTORNEY

"This beautiful tale of triumph can be enjoyed by and beneficial to people from all walks of life, no matter who they are or what their circumstances in life happen to be."-

GARY BABINEAUX, ENTERPRENEUR

TWO NICKELS
AND A DIME

What a difference three hours can make…

TWO NICKELS AND A DIME

LYNDON LIVINGSTON

5L PUBLISHING

5 L Publishing PO Box 778
Kinder, LA 70648
1-337-738-8280

Published in the USA
ISBN: 9781545220931

Acknowledgement and Thanks

Thanks to a special wife who helped and prayed for this project. Thanks, Paula for your ideas, your prayers, and your love.

Thanks to a special man who planted so many seeds in me many years ago. What you read is not only my story, it is a story he made possible by his total commitment to Jesus. Thanks Brother Bob Stamps.

This book is dedicated to a true seed planter who was a very dear friend to me and all those who were in need. John Burton now smiles from heaven to see the fruit of all the seeds he planted.

INTRODUCTION

This book is about a challenge that faces each of us, not only as individuals, but also as a country as a whole. It is about many of my personal learning experiences, but more so, about what God has led me to do and say. It is not however, a book about me, but rather a book about you. It is a travel with me and 'Two Nickels And A Dime' to a point where I was led to offer you a personal challenge that is a very unique approach to grace and you.

This approach to grace is issued to all people. Everyone, from housewife to businessman, will benefit and be able to incorporate the challenge into their lives. Once there, it will transform everyone in all areas of their lives. There are no areas of anyone's life that cannot succeed if they accept the challenge. Whether young or old, the struggles will fade. It truly will guarantee success whether it be in the area of relationships, financial issues, health issues, depression, loneliness, or business walls to climb. Success is guaranteed not because it was written by me, but because God stands behind every word of it.

This unique grace approach, that I term the 'Three Hour Challenge', is an avenue for spiritual and personal growth in many ways. It transcends denominational lines, gender lines, age lines, political ideological lines, social economic lines, geographic boundaries and all other lines that would separate us. The 'Three Hour Challenge' can be taken by individuals, groups, and churches, but in the end, it is all about *you*! There are no steps or lists. It is that one person acting!

This 'Three Hour Challenge' is simply put, a program of giving back grace. If people in this country, will accept the challenge, lives will be changed. Truly, America itself will be changed!

Contents

Chapter 1
The Double I Got At Wendy's
That I Didn't Order...

This day in 2013 seemed so predictable which was not uncommon. Really, don't we spend our whole lifetime trying to get into the "ruts" of life, and then most certainly we complain about how things never change? We seek routine and then complain of boredom. I had certainly followed this routine so many times before. There would be the drive from my hometown of Kinder, Louisiana, which was a small town of about 2,500 people to a larger town, Lake Charles, Louisiana. Guess I was destined to live in small-town, USA. I only had two real hometowns of any consequence in my life. There was Kinder, where I live now, and a small east Texas town, named San Augustine, where I spent most of my childhood. It's somewhat puzzling how people always believe that their small town is unique and special. And yet, in all towns, not just ours, there seems to be so many commonalities. This seems true, not only with towns, but especially with the people who live there. We tend to view our small town neighbors as good people who will step up when the chips are down. They will take care of each other, even though everyone knows everyone else's business. And, an occasional discourse with its root in local politics will raise its ugly head, but that too fades. After all, we say over and over, our town is a good place to live. Makes you wonder about those other small towns, like the ones that are our arch rivals in sports. Are they good towns with good people? And those large towns and cities are constantly in the news because of their troubles. What kind of people live there? I don't really know why I was thinking about towns and people that day. I guess it was as good a way as any to fill the time as I drove. I mean, really, I finally concluded, people are people and you pretty much can predict how they will react to just about anything. You smile, they smile. You mention their child, they light up. Someone dies, they cry. You ask people how they are doing, they say fine. You order a double at Wendy's, you get a hamburger with two meat patties. Yep, people and most everything else are pretty predictable. The drive was not very far from Kinder to Lake Charles, only about thirty-five miles. I planned a stop by which to eat an early lunch and then to play a round of golf at the local golf course. Somedays, however, stand out as very special in a person's life and this would be a very memorable day. But at Wendy's? I mean, really, a special day at a fast food joint? Only a very big God can make that happen!

This particular day was going very much according to script, as I entered the Wendy's at the corner of Loop 210 and Highway 14. As I said before, don't most days and most people follow script? It was early and consequently there were few people in Wendy's. As I approached the counter to order, I noticed the person working the order station. She was a strikingly beautiful young black lady. She was probably in her early twenties with a sincere smile that made you feel welcomed. I was the only person in line and I placed my order with her. As I finished, the young lady said to me, "I know you." My mind immediately kicked into high gear. Like most people, I find it so uncomfortable when a person knows you and you can't recall their name. I knew that I had seen her before, but I simply couldn't recall the name or place where I had seen her. She was too young to be one of my former students. I had taught history and coached football for twenty years but I had retired too many years prior for her to have been one of my students. Ashamedly, I said, "I'm so sorry, but I ....". In a very soft voice, she interrupted me, "Well, I don't know your name, but I do know what you did." Her tone had become more serene and displayed a faint hint of emotion. Wow, my mind was certainly racing now. What did she know that I had done? I had no extramarital affairs, wasn't gay, hadn't stolen anything, or didn't beat my kids. What did I do? Seemingly, it must have been really bad for this beautiful young lady to remember an older, common looking guy like me. Funny, how we always assume the worst. She obviously could see the confusion on my face as she continued, "You were in here about two weeks ago." Again, my mind was leap frogging back in time. Yes, I suddenly remembered that indeed I had been in two weeks prior. But again, why would she remember me? She obviously waits on hundreds of people each day. As she continued, I finally realized where she was going with the story. I let her tell me the story, but now I remembered. "That day", she continued, "you came in and ordered your meal. You sat over there and ate". She pointed to the dining area where indeed I had sat. "While you were eating, an old black man came in. He was really looking bad. I mean, this guy was dirty, and really looked like he was homeless." As she continued with her story, I saw tears begin to swell ever so slightly in the young lady's eyes. For sure, I now knew where this story was going, but I couldn't speak, so I let her finish the story. "You finished eating your meal and this old man had sat at a table by the door on the other side of the room. You then approached the order counter and asked our manager who was standing there if we sold gift cards. Our manager said, "Yes, we do". You told her that you would like one for twenty dollars and she brought you the gift card. She then asked if you wanted an envelope. Again, you said you did. Our manager stepped away as she handed you the gift card in the envelope. You then asked if you could borrow my pen. By now, I was looking intently at the young lady. I was not only amazed that she remembered all these details, but I was captured by the emotion and raw feelings she displayed as she recalled the events. The tears in her eyes were now more pronounced, and I still couldn't speak. As we looked into each other's eyes, it felt as though our very souls had met. We were so very opposite. And yet, at that point in time, it was almost as if we were one. Totally opposite, a young beautiful black lady and an older, common, white man and yet for now, we had transcended the boundaries of age, race and gender. Our hearts had truly met at a common place. She continued the story in an even quieter voice, "I gave you my pen, and you turned away to write on the envelope. You didn't know it, but I peeked at what you wrote. On the envelope, you wrote, 'God Loves You'." I couldn't respond because I knew I would cry so I simply nodded and bit the inside of my lips to keep the tears inside. She was wiping the tears from her eyes now as she finished the story. "You took the envelope over to the old man and told him what it was and gave it to him. Then, you just patted him on his shoulder and left." This was all true. The old man had simply looked up at me and smiled. But I knew, he had understood. *It's funny how people always remember what you do so much more than what you say.* I knew at that instance that the seed of 'loving the unlovable' that had been planted that fateful day two weeks before would be manifest in that young lady for the rest of her life. I thought I knew what I was doing when I planted that seed of discipleship that I call 'loving the unlovable'. I thought I was planting that seed in an old unlovable, homeless looking man. But as God would have it, it was actually planted as well in the young lady. I do know this with certainty- someday, in some way, that young lady will plant her own seed of 'loving the unlovable'. Probably, she will do so many, many times over. And who knows, perhaps, she will plant that seed with me, you, my children or your children. I'm not certain where, how, when, or with whom. I'm only certain that she will. The seed is now hers to share. She will 'love the unlovable'! If I had given the old man the gift card without writing anything on it, that would have simply been an act of kindness, but it is amazing how three little words, 'God Loves You', changed everything. I've been back to that Wendy's many times since that day, and have never seen that sweet young lady since. But she and I will always share something special. So you see, at Wendy's, I believed I had, in a small way, offered a blessing to an old homeless-looking man, when in fact, the blessing came to all three of us, who seemingly were worlds apart in every way- the old man, the young lady and especially me. I didn't eat my double meat burger that day, but I did get a double portion. Wendy's didn't serve it though, God did! I got in my truck that day, and as I left Wendy's, I wept…

THOUGHTS

- 'Loving the unlovable' is a seed of discipleship that *always* blesses the giver and the receiver.

- Once given to someone else, seeds of discipleship are replanted many times over.

- People always remember what we do so much more than what we say.

- The snapping shrimp can produce a sound louder than a jet engine…what we do can be just as explosive.

Chapter 2
Those Smelly Hospitals....

I didn't get far at all as I left Wendy's that day. It really wasn't because of the tears. My tears were not the sobbing, choking kind that keeps you from catching your breath and consequently would have kept me from driving. No, these were gentle, flowing tears. Along with them was a certain calmness. I realized that I really just needed to gather my thoughts. So it was, that I traveled the whole distance of one block. I then drove into the Wal-Mart parking lot that was adjacent to the Wendy's. As I stopped my truck and rested my head on the steering wheel, I knew it was not in order to stop the tears. It truly was to eliminate the clutter and let my mind travel down a path it was more familiar with.

Very often when we plant a seed of 'loving the unlovable', we believe we are giving a blessing to the one we are planting the seed with. And, that is true. But, there is also a very real blessing for the one who is giving the blessing, the one who gives back the grace they have received in their life. Too often we believe our reward will be in heaven. And surely that is true. But I am a witness many times over that blessings, rewards, and favor are for here and now on this earth. We don't have to wait until heaven for our reward. Just as Mark 10:29-30 tells us, our reward is here on earth and not only when we die but *now*. I'm sure because I received one on this day. Our blessings are immediate even though the manifestation of those blessings may come later in many ways. Oh, what blessings!

Jesus said, "Truly, I say to you, there is no one who has left house or brothers or sisters or mother or father or children or lands, for my sake and for the gospel, who will not receive a hundredfold now in this time, houses and brothers and sisters and mothers and children and lands, with persecutions, and in the age to come eternal life".

The blessing that day was not only what I was 'feeling'. It was the assurance that the seed of 'loving the unlovable' was now planted in a young lady and an old man.

For me, the seeds that I plant in my lifetime are my legacy. Everyone leaves a legacy. It is so sad that often when some of us leave this world, our legacy consists of a stone grave marker with a short epitaph. What legacy do even the most famous leave behind such as the movie stars, billionaires, and rock stars? They are remembered for a season. The seeds we plant are not only what we are giving the world at the present time, but also what we are leaving behind, our legacy. I am firmly convinced that they will exist long after we are gone.

I have a group of friends from another state that I share a common interest with. We play dominoes together, usually tournament play. Even though we are hundreds of miles apart, we get together frequently and fellowship. To a man, they always call me "the luckiest man alive". When they say that I always chuckle deep down. I choose to believe that I am not lucky. I choose to believe that I am simply reaping the harvest from planting the seeds. I am enjoying the favor of the Lord.

He doesn't leave me even when I play dominoes. No matter if I am enjoying a sporting event or facing a grave struggle, I always expect a harvest. After all, when a farmer plants seeds, doesn't he expect a harvest? I have learned that when we give, it is alright to expect a return.

Like most people, I have certainly come face to face with struggles and troubles. I have learned first-hand though, that if we plant a seed when we are hurting, the blessing will follow. In fact, by planting seeds we are actually planting for the struggles that lie *ahead* in our life. Blessings are like prayer in some respects. The timing for both should be left up to God. He is the one that has the perfect plan. He knows the perfect who, what, when, and where.

From time to time, we all probably imagine what it will be like when we meet our Lord in heaven. I always imagine the Lord sitting with me, taking my hands in his nail scarred hands, and looking into my eyes with those piercing eyes. He might ask me about my time on earth. I don't want to have to say, "Lord, I would have read the Bible more, but that's pretty hard stuff to understand." I believe that would cause His eyes to become tearful. I don't want to have to add, "Lord, I would have attended church more often, but I just was so busy with life and all". I know that would cause His tears to flow. And I never want to say," Lord, I didn't pray much because I just didn't feel comfortable talking to you especially with people around, even my wife and family". I know at that moment my Lord's grief would be obvious. What I want to be able to tell the Lord is about the seeds I planted in His name. There will be no tears in my Lord's eyes at that moment. He will smile the biggest smile imaginable. He might let out a big roar of laughter. I want so much for Him to tell me, "You did good son, you did good". *I also believe that Jesus is going to show me all the places that my seeds went, the lives they affected, and the blessings that came from them.*

Emotional and tearful most assuredly are not common traits for a person who had spent his entire professional life trying to stay calm and in control. This wasn't a first down or a personal foul penalty though. This was real life events that leave lasting impressions for a lifetime. Stopping the tears was simply a matter of a couple of deep breaths, coupled with a groan or two. The thoughts, however were now in fast forward mode. My mind was really seeking the answer to the question that seemed to shout from my soul. Why do I do the things I do? Usually I never intend to plant a seed. They just happen. Why? Over the years, I had planted many seeds of discipleship by 'loving the unlovable'. But, I really felt deeply moved by this particular time. Why this time? Was it because of the people involved? Was it just an emotional time for me? Trying to find the answer, I traveled back in time...a long, long way back in time...

It was a cold winter day, and I was so very glad to be playing in a junior high basketball game. I knew full well that if I didn't have that game to play, I would be working in the fields. Even though I was only in the seventh grade, I was needed in the fields as much as possible. My family was one of the poorest of the poor in San Augustine County and everyone was needed every day to meet the need...not the need of a new car, nor new clothes, nor new anything, just the absolute need of subsistence.

My three boys today have no idea what I'm really trying to get them to understand when I tell them we were poor. They are like most kids… no, like most people today. They don't know that kind of poverty that we faced in those days. I learned as a young boy growing up in the watermelon fields of east Texas what real poverty was. Poverty is not just an absence of money or material possessions. It goes deeper. It is feelings. It is emotions. And it is very real to the person experiencing it. Poverty is something that is truly difficult to understand unless you actually have experienced it. In many ways, poverty has much in common with cancer. Both are devastating to the mind, body, and spirit. And yet, no one really understands either unless they have been there. I have felt the sting of both and hope you never do. But the poverty of my youth was very real. Playing all my junior high football games barefooted because we couldn't afford tennis shoes didn't bother me, but the pointing and laughing from the other team did. Having to walk home from school because we certainly couldn't afford a vehicle for me didn't bother me, but the snickers from some of the other kids did. The holes in my jeans didn't bother me, but the look on the grownups faces as they glanced at my jeans did. The doing without was bad for sure, but the worse part of poverty was the way many people made me feel. I don't believe it was an intentionally mean-spirited action on their part but rather a learned response to a condition that they had gleaned from society. Poverty truly is a feeling. I say that now, not to have people feel sorry for me, but to give people something to think about the next time they see a kid with uncut hair, a t-shirt that is way too big, ragged jeans, or so on. You get the idea. *Poverty is given to children...so can grace be given.*

I'm not sure if there was government welfare in those days. I do know that we didn't receive any if it did exist. That is not to insinuate that we wouldn't have taken the help. I assume we were just too uninformed to know about it or how to get it, since no one in my family had ever even graduated from high school.

Indeed, I was very glad to have a basketball game to play that day. Usually, I couldn't miss work for basketball but today was different since it was cold and rainy anyway. But then again, I don't believe that things happen just by chance. God's plan is always in place and always perfectly timed.

Ordinarily the only time I was excused from work in the fields was for football. I assume that's one of the reasons I started at an early age to love that game so much. It was fun, but it was also a "get out of work free" card for me. But this day, it was basketball. I really don't remember the game. I can't tell you which team we were playing. I don't know the score. I do remember a fast break, a group of us going up for the ball, and I remember the horrific pain as I came down on the ball, as it lay on the floor. My head and back were really in pain. And looking back, I'm so glad! That fast break fiasco changed my life forever!

The pain in my head and back seemed inconsequential compared to the smell of the hospital. Not that the smell of the San Augustine Hospital was any different than the smell of any other hospital. It was just that I remembered that unique smell and the nausea that would overcome me when I encountered it. That is true even to this day. I had never been a patient in a hospital. But I knew that distinctive aroma that made me so ill. Each time I had gone to visit my mother in the hospital four years earlier I had been met with that horrible smell. My mother never came out of that hospital. She passed away when I was ten years old. She was only thirty-seven years old when cancer took her life. For a ten-year-old, death is a hard thing to understand. A mother's death is even more uniquely hard to grasp. I still remember many things about my mother. I recall the long hours she, as a single parent, was away from home because she worked as a waitress at a local restaurant. I remember the hugs she would give me and how they made me feel oh so special. I remember how she cared for me when I was sick. I remember much about her. But the thing I remember most is how even though I was young, she always listened to me. Consequently, I learned early in life that the simple act of listening is a powerful force. Yes, it was as though she was listening to my heart. She always knew what I was really feeling regardless of what my words were. Mothers always know, don't they?

My mother and my father were divorced and I was so crushed when she passed away. After her death, I went to live with my father in San Augustine. I guess some things never change… I still love my mother and I still can't stand the smell of hospitals.

The doctor's diagnosis for my injury was a sprained back which called for a week of traction. I remember thinking that traction would be okay, but I needed help with… you guessed it, the smell.

Looking back, now, I really have a deeper understanding of

all that has happened to me. To me, it is apparent that God had a plan and now I am confident that we always come out in our place of abundance. (Psalms 66:12)

"You sent troops to ride across our broken bodies. We went through fire and flood. But in the end, you brought us into wealth and great abundance".

And as God would have it, my place of abundance was about to appear. I had been lying in that hospital bed for two days when the door slowly opened around noon of the third day. Expecting to see a doctor or nurse, instead I was met with a sheepish grin from a young man probably in his late twenties. He wore rounded spectacles and was already balding even at that early age. As his eyes met mine, a huge smile appeared on his face. "Can I come in, Brother?" the young man asked. I noticed he was dressed much different than common folks in San Augustine. I for sure thought he must be a lawyer. "Sure", I replied. "My name is Bob Stamps", he began. "I am the youth director at the local Methodist church." The smile never left his face as he talked. We talked at length about real life topics such as school, and school activities. I guess that was about all we could talk about. I didn't know God stuff and he didn't know sports. I don't remember the topic transition, but soon he was talking about the Bible and Jesus. I could actually feel the excitement in his voice when he spoke of Jesus. I guess that is true of many young pastors or youth directors. However, over the years, subsequent to that hospital visit, that excitement has never left Brother Bob. Bob would leave San Augustine after a couple of years to go to Oral Roberts University as the Chaplain, but he never lost his noticeable excitement about

Jesus. And wherever he has gone, he is simply known as 'Brother Bob'. Those two facts will always be true whether he is at ORU, Asbury Seminary, or a smelly hospital room in San Augustine, Texas... he is 'Brother Bob' and he is excited about Jesus. What a great way to be remembered, not by title, job description, or status in life, but rather as "Brother 'Anybody' who is still excited about Jesus"! Now that is a true legacy! And that's the man standing in my hospital room sharing this story of Jesus with a young kid who had little knowledge and less understanding. In retrospect, I am so glad that he didn't think like so many people would. He didn't judge me as many might today and probably did then. Imagine, one kid who had no idea about Christianity and didn't come from a churched family. Some, maybe even some preachers, might consider that a "lot of sugar for a dime". No, he didn't dismiss me. He didn't just give me a courtesy call inviting me to church. No, he didn't excuse himself and leave to speak to Rotary or some other large group where more people would hear his message. He was willing to invest his time and energy in one kid. *He was willing to invest of himself in one worthless kid who would never be able to repay him for his time, energy, and compassion.* He understood the miracle of seed planting.

This story that I was hearing was new and exciting to me, although I had vaguely heard of some of the characters before. I knew the name, Jesus, but I didn't understand what that name meant or could mean to me. My family didn't attend church, and I never really wondered why. I guess, you could say our poverty extended to the spiritual realm. Looking back at my childhood, I have often wondered why we were so spiritually void considering it seemed there was a church on every corner in our town. Where were all those church going Christians? Of all the things I have to say, I sincerely believe, we need to ask again, for not only then but even today, where were/are all those church going Christians? Think about it.

I do know and knew then, that this man standing before me, and sharing the story of Jesus with me was truly a Christian. You could surely tell that it wasn't something he just talked about. This was something that he was driven to live out. The story he told was the one that probably we've all heard, the story of how Christ died on the cross for each of us. I distinctly remember that the hardest part of this story to believe was that I, the poorest of the poor, the most undeserving of people, could have this gift of Christ's redemption free!

Brother Bob explained it all so well, but really???? Free ???? To me???? I tried to remember if anyone had ever given me anything for free. Aren't we all told that there are "no free lunches", and that "you get what you work for"? But this young youth director was assuring me that it was free to me and that not only did I not have to work to get it, but that I couldn't get it by working for it. And then, he looked at me, and said, still with a smile on his face, "Brother, I can share with you the story, but you are the one who has to make the decision of what it is you would like to do."

Later on in life, when I was a football coach, I would always tell our team that they had to really be ready and play hard every single play because even though the game was four quarters, forty-eight minutes, the fate of the game was usually decided by no more than one or two plays. Those were the crucial plays that more likely than not determined the outcome of the game. I realize now that at that moment I was facing that crucial play in the game of life. As I looked into Brother Bob's eyes, I knew in my heart the decision that I needed and wanted to make. He took my hand as we prayed, and it was one of those decisions that determined the fate of my life forever. I'm sure that there is always joy in a person's heart when they accept Jesus as their Savior, but I tell you that I experienced a joy out of control! Think of where I had been. I was among the poorest of the poor, most undeserving, wretched soul and now I was the son of the most-high God! I now shared in riches unspeakable! From that day until now, I have always believed that I am wealthy and that I share in all the goodness and prosperity that my God has! Imagine what I had, and what I now had because of that one day or play in that game called, 'life' when I said 'yes' to a Savior who offered. Immediately, I went from being a pauper to being a King's son! *The poverty of my life was now conquered by grace.* Actually, I didn't have more money or wealth but I was free from all poverty. From that day until now, I have never felt poor again. And that has made all the difference.

THOUGHTS

- Poverty is given to children…so can grace be given.

- Listening is a powerful force.

- We always come out of anything in our place of abundance.

- Our reward is on Earth and it is in the present tense, now.

- Being poor is not about the absence of wealth. It is more about the feelings and emotions that accompany it.

- The most valuable thing in existence is free, salvation.

Chapter 3
Never Know What You Will Find
Down Old Dusty Dirt Roads...

My tears had now stopped as I looked around the parking lot where my truck had some to rest. Somehow, my mind had seemingly reset. A sigh from deep within signaled the end of the emotional flood that I had felt since leaving Wendy's. The reliving of my hospital experience, whereby I accepted Jesus as my Lord, that had occurred so many years prior had apparently been a great catalyst for clearing my mind and gave me a great peace. The peace I felt was so surreal that instead of driving off that Wal-Mart parking lot, I just sat quietly and listened to my heart. I felt that I still had not fully answered the question that I so wanted an answer to, "Why do I do the things I do?", such as planting the seed of discipleship of which 'loving the unlovable' is an example! So with this on my mind, my heart took me further down memory lane.

Following my hospital experience in which Brother Bob led me to the Lord, it was a most memorable two years. I learned more in those two years about Christian living, real Christian living, than in every book I've ever read. There were Bible studies, prayer time, witnessing time, church services, but above all, time to see the Christian life 'real-time'. When I use the term 'real-time' I'm referring to the everyday people we meet who have very real issues and struggles that they are facing. These are the people who are in need of seed planting by real-time Christians.

Perhaps too many of us reside in a spiritual world that relies on the past too much. When I hear people tell of how their grandfather was one of the founding fathers, or "put the first shingle" on this or that church, I think how sad that is. They usually say it with such pride and I certainly am not opposed to being proud of family history. That is a good thing. But too often it appears that that is the place in time where their spiritual life is stuck. It appears that is the shining accomplishment of their own Christian being. You see, I don't want to simply know what their grandfather did. I want to talk to them about the exciting things they are doing *today* that is just as important as that first shingle on the church roof. Some are just not in real time but 'past' time. Then we have the Christians who are stuck in the future. With them it is like the old sermon, 'payday-someday'. I refer to them as 'heavenites'. They are waiting on heaven for all good things to happen. But for me the favor of the Lord Jesus is for now and not just for when we die. So yes, I strive to be a 'real-time' believer. There is a place for the past and a place for the future, but I aspire to be in the now. Being in the now also gives us a chance to meet people at their need. So if we are in the real-time, we can meet and minister to people who have real-time issues. Their issues and struggles are very real. The test is our ability to get in the 'now' with them.

People facing the challenges of life don't need someone to

only tell them that everything is going to be great once we get to heaven. If you don't have a job because of a recession and consequently can't take your child to see a doctor, you really don't need a talk about heaven. You need someone who is in real-time. If you are crushed because you've learned that your child is hooked on drugs, you don't need someone to only tell you about what a great church they attend and how they've been attending services there for thirty years. You don't just need an invitation to church. You need someone who will be in real-time and who will hold your hand, pray *with* you not just *for* you, and yes maybe even cry with you because they are willing to share the pain. Perhaps, this was the greatest lesson that I learned during this time. We did have great Bible studies. Even if there was no one else available, Brother Bob and I would study the scripture together. Maybe a thirty-thousand-person congregation is not what's really needed. Perhaps we need more one on one interactions. Just saying...

I learned so much about the Bible in those days. We also had great prayer times. Again, even if there was no one else there, we would still pray. I learned so much about praying, not about memorizing prayers nor saying what I might think sounds good, but about really just talking to God. After all, He is my Father! I realize now that God was using all this time and fellowship to plant seeds in my life that would last forever. However, again I would offer that perhaps the greatest lesson was the 'real-time' lesson I learned about being a true Christian, how do we treat people, not just the ones that look like us, talk like us, think like us... but all people, real-time! All that being said, I certainly in no way would minimize the lessons from the

Bible. I firmly believe we get much of our spiritual growth from studying the Word. We should know about how God created everything; how He parted the Red Sea; how Jesus raised the dead; how He healed the lame, and the list goes on. But what I did also learn was that we need to be able to look people in the eye and know their pain when they tell about being ill, about their hurt when they tell about not being able to pay their rent, about the devastation they feel since their spouse's betrayal, and about how they feel since being placed in the assisted living facility. That's what I call real-time Christianity.

I learned so much from the time I spent in San Augustine County and the seeds of discipleship that were planted in me during this time that would be replanted by me into others many times throughout my lifetime. For many of the seeds of discipleship, I don't remember a very specific event or time in which it was planted within me. For one seed however, I very specifically recall the very memorable time it was planted.

It was a Sunday afternoon. I don't remember much about the morning service at church that day. In rethinking the day, it is highly likely that it was a service whereby the Lord was greatly served. Over the years, I have often reminisced about the pastors that led not only our church but also some of the other churches in our area. I remember some spirit led men who were totally committed to the Lord.

Very rural area, sparsely populated, generally under educated populous- sounds just like a place that my God wants to be! And indeed, he was present on this particular Sunday.

It was nearing dusk as Brother Bob and I rounded the curve on an old dusty, dirt road. We had gone to do a home visit that afternoon and were returning home in order to get ready for the evening worship service. In those days, evening services still existed. I am not sure why we don't have evening services anymore. Maybe we just don't have time for such.

If you have ever driven down a dirt road, in rural east Texas, you understand how a cloud of dust bellows from behind the vehicle. Nothing escapes the heavy dust cloud that builds as the vehicle moves along the dirt road. Anything or anybody behind, gets the wrath of the dust cloud. Likewise, whatever lies ahead is bathed in the dust as the traveling vehicle passes.

As I glanced in the side mirror, I could see that there was no recipient of our dust cloud being produced by the car we were in. We were now slowing as we approached the stop sign ahead. The dirt road would thankfully come to a dead end at the stop sign, and we would finally be on a farm-to-market road, Highway 711. As we came to a stop, the dirt cloud passed us and enveloped our car and everything ahead in its path. As the dust began to clear and moved past, I noticed a silhouette of a person standing across the road. When the dust was finally gone, I could clearly see a person standing on the shoulder of the road. Even to this day, I can still detail the old man who was standing there looking straight at us. His clothes were filthy. He was wearing an old camouflaged jacket. This man was one of the most hideous looking people that I had ever seen. I was sure his graying beard and hair had never been washed. The backpack lying by him told me that he was probably homeless. As Brother Bob turned the car from the old dirt road onto Highway 711, I blurted out to him, "Holy cow! Did you see that guy? He was like the ugliest creature I have ever laid eyes on. I mean, he was gross." And then, one of the greatest things to ever happen to me occurred. It was a most unforgettable moment for me. Brother Bob looked over at me and said, "Lyndon, if that had been a movie star or a great professional athlete, what would have been your reaction then?" Of course I was taken aback. I felt great conviction and guilt for my reaction to the old man. In my heart, I knew if that had been a movie star or professional athlete, I would have been in awe and would have wanted an autograph. But truth is, this old man was as much a creation of God, and deserved grace as much as, any movie star. He was in fact 'real-time'. And then, Brother Bob planted the seed and probably didn't even know it as he continued, "Lyndon, you have to learn to *love the unlovable*." And what a change that has made in my life and how I view people. I have attempted to replant that seed of discipleship that I now call 'loving the unlovables' many times, and hopefully it has been passed on by others.

As I drove out of the Wal-Mart parking lot, I felt a real contentment with my day, partly because of my Wendy's experience and partly because my trip down memory lane reminded me of where I had come from and where God had brought me.

I've driven by that Wendy's many times in the past three years since my experience there, and most assuredly I always think to myself.... "Love the Unlovable." And I do know why I do what I do! It's all because someone cared enough to plant that seed in me all those years ago...

THOUGHTS

- Our focus should be to live the Christian life 'real-time'.

- The true measure of greatness is how we treat people... *all people*.

- We must be able to 'love the unlovable' no matter what they look like.

- A mole is small but it can dig a 300 foot tunnel in one night. We may think of ourselves as but one individual. However, we too can produce explosive results.

Chapter 4

Lunacy or Heresy...

In the first three chapters of this book, I have attempted to set the background for what I believe, and why I do the things I do. It's all about the seeds that God has planted in me. But the real purpose of this book is not to offer my personal testimony. It's about us...we...all of us individually. There are certain clichés we have all heard probably for our entire life, such as 'America is going to hell in a handbasket'; 'young people today have no respect for anything, 'the whole world is heading down a treacherous path toward oblivion quickly'; 'people just don't care anymore'; 'If America doesn't change, God is going to turn his back on America' (This seems to be a favorite of many television evangelists). And the list goes on. Perhaps, we need to be extraordinarily careful in characterizing America as being under God's judgment and condemnation. That is precisely what the terrorist groups are saying about America. Think about that. Do we really agree with the terrorists about America?

As Christians, we all want to be better people. We want a better country. But honestly, we just don't really know how to get there. We most often feel hopeless when it comes to our country. We also feel that our people themselves are just not spiritual enough. Of course, that is those *other* people. It's not us. If everyone else would just change, maybe so would our country. Yep, those *other* people need to change. Recently I've spent much time praying, thinking, and studying about this. This presidential election cycle has really heightened my perception of what I believe to be happening in our country, and more importantly, in our lives.

Candidates are angry, people are upset, differences of opinion escalate to conflict, and tension exists between people for the most inconsequential of reasons. Wow! Maybe, we do need to ask ourselves, 'Is America going to hell in a handbasket'? After all, many of the television evangelists tell us that we have turned our back on God as a nation and that a day of reckoning is fast approaching. We have removed prayer from our schools, approved of same-sex marriages, approved of abortions, and disallowed the display of the Ten Commandments on public grounds. This attack on Christian principles seems to grow daily. I would offer that most Christians across our country agree that these are hugely problematic and need to be addressed.

So, how do we solve these problems and as one prominent politician likes to say, "make America great again"? Let me say from the onset, that this is not a political discourse. It is rather written about you and me individually. However, let's look at us from a broader perspective. I have questioned many recently about this question of how to make America the country we desire it to be, a country guided by Christian principles and thus laws that support and not tear down those principles. Inevitably, the response to this question comes from one of two camps. I would note that the responses are the same whether talking to clergy or masses. It appears that the answer is so obvious to these two camps of people. However, as we see in Job 11:1-20, what men see may not be what God means. Job's friends were absolutely sure that Job must have sinned greatly for the catastrophes that he was facing to have occurred. What his friends thought was obvious was not true at all and certainly did not represent the intent of God. I have prayed much for our country, and now I am convinced that we must look beyond the obvious. Remember, this is all about us individually, not about a country.

The first response I get when asking people about how to change this country into the country it should be is that we need to elect good, Christian, God-fearing people to office. With the right people in political office, things will change for the better is the theory. For sure, I am on board that we should attempt to elect Christian people to office. But, the idea that Christian men or women will steer our country in the right direction when elected to office has many gaps in the theory. It appears when extrapolating from the past that often results can't be foretold with great accuracy in all cases. Abraham Lincoln was a licensed bartender. Grover Cleveland held the job of hangman. Andrew Jackson taught his parrot to curse. John Adam's campaign literature stated that if Thomas Jefferson was elected,"murder, robbery, rape, adultery, and incest will be openly taught and practiced." Rutherford Hayes banished alcohol from the White House and held gospel sing-alongs every night in the White House. Can we tell from their credentials which would make the best leader for our country? Was Rutherford Hayes the best of the mentioned political leaders? Did he do the most for mankind? I'm convinced that during his time as a public official, Thomas Jefferson was considered a fine Christian man. As a history teacher, I can tell you he was one of my favorite presidents. Who couldn't like Thomas Jefferson? Here was a man, who by his own proclamation believed in God. He is credited with writing most of the Declaration of Independence. He believed in the ability of the common man to run the government, and fought against the big national bank. Sounds good.

Jefferson didn't believe in slavery. Even though he was a slave owner, he freed many of his slaves, and never had one pursued that escaped. Additionally, he did much more that would qualify him for that period of time as a good, moral person. Yet, as a leader, Thomas Jefferson also published his own Bible. Still sounds like a good Christian leader, huh? Upon closer look, we can see in Jefferson's Bible, he left out the virgin birth. He also left out any acknowledgment of miracles that were performed. He concluded with the death of Christ but never mentioned the resurrection. So the Christian leader that the people elected, and I am not judging whether Jefferson was a Christian or not, perhaps was different than the one who helped run the government. Makes me wonder if Christians today would even vote for him? The point being that to attempt to elect good Christian people to office is much more complex and often does not produce the results we desire and even perhaps produces results we would not have imagined. I am not sure about Jefferson's Christian values, but I am convinced he was a good political leader.

Would liberal Democratic political leaders be acceptable?

Or would conservative Republican leaders be acceptable? Sometimes, when I listen to some Christians, I think that they must believe that God is a Republican and naturally Satan is a Democrat. Then, I talk to other people and they are convinced that God is a Democrat and Satan is a Republican. Come on, God, are you riding the fence on us?

Truth is, I don't think God looks at politics like we do at all. I believe that God doesn't view politics as the *answer* to a world gone awry. Furthermore, the morals of a people cannot me legislated. They are from within. The morals and standards of a nation come from its people. Politicians can't legislate our people or our country as a body to be moral. Morals and even laws and practices that dictate morals don't trickle down from politicians to the people, but rather *flow upward from the people to the governing bodies* in the form of politicians. Our entire system of government is formed on the basis of the consent of the governed. We get the laws and rules that germinate from the actions of our people, our everyday people, not politicians. If there are enough good Christian people, there will be good Christian politicians. Consequently, I think God is more concerned about you and me, the people, and not the politicians.

The only real solution to our dilemma does not rest with the laws dictated by politicians or even interpretations of those laws by our political judicial system. We, as Christians, should certainly understand the principle that the issue is not the law. It's about the grace within each of us. By now, we as Christians should be acutely aware that the issue of laws versus grace has been settled. It started with Adam and Eve. They were given a good, simple law... eat of any fruit from any tree you wish except one. On all the earth, they could choose fruit from any tree, except that one. That's any easy law that they should be able to obey...they failed. Maybe, if they would have elected the right president, they could change their law... How about the Jewish nation? They were given really good laws. They were simple. As a matter of fact, God reduced it to ten, The Ten Commandments. That's easy enough... the Jewish nation failed. Maybe, they needed a more conservative president too....

I remember a humorous event concerning the law that happened to me as a football coach. For the longest, I had struggled with team rules. What should they be and how should they be stated was my dilemma. I was at a conference one day and I heard a nationally recognized coach telling about how he always expected his team to do the right thing no matter where they were. Then and there, it dawned on me. That is my team law. One rule, "Do Right". That was so simple that all our players could understand that. I figured that was simple and after all, our players would know right from wrong in light of the fact that they were in high school. I never had a player question me about whether something was right or wrong. Young people are so much brighter than any of us give them credit for. That being said, I did have some players from time to time, who didn't do right. However, they always understood the issue was them and their behavior, not the rule. Those who didn't do right would have to do what we termed, "Do Rights" after practice. A "Do Right" was a one-hundred-yard sprint with a somersault every five yards, not fun. One day, a player who had transgressed was ready to accept his "do rights" when he asked me, "Hey, Coach, what about that 'forgiveness' thing? I thought a minute and then told him, "It's right next to that 'consequences' thing, and you're getting both." We both laughed and at least he got a chuckle out of his 'do rights'. I am not sure his chuckle was sincere though.

So I would offer that we should stop blaming the politicians and perhaps look in the mirror! And that brings me to the second response I always get when asking the question about what it will take to make this country great again.

Recall, the first response people give is to elect good, Christian people to office. The second response is that we need to get down on our knees and pray for this country and its leaders. If you doubt these responses, try asking people that you know what they think this country needs to do to be great again. I tell you with certainty, that most if not all, will say either that we need to elect good people to office or they will reply that we need to pray this country back to greatness. I recently had lunch with a pastor and a retired pastor. After lunch, I asked both the question, and the retired pastor replied that we need to overhaul our political system by getting good people into positions where they can help our country. In other words, he felt we need a good president, a decent God-fearing Supreme Court, and a Congress that is based on good Biblical principles. To get there he offered that we needed to elect the right kind of people. I then turned to the pastor and asked him if he agreed, or if he had a different idea on what we needed. His response was that what we desperately needed was prayer for our country and its leaders. He stated that God answers prayers and would honor our request. I thanked both for their sincerity. And then I told them what I offer now. I believe both to be wrong in their approach. I know... I know...it sounds like a marriage of lunacy and heresy to say that electing Christians to political office will not work and to further say that prayer will not be the answer either. However, that's what I'm saying! Please, don't throw down the book yet. Let me offer more. As I have explained, the election of Christians to office is not the answer for a variety of reasons. We may end up with people like Thomas Jefferson, not that he was a bad person or President, but certainly not what we would have imagined as a good Christian by today's standard. Did that make him a bad President?

And then comes the heresy. Prayer is not the answer? Come on! Can't prayer solve all problems? Prayer can solve problems, no matter how big. Remember when Zerubbabel faced great problems in rebuilding the temple and Zachariah told him that the Lord says to say, "Grace, grace" to your mountains and they will become a plain. We are told for sure, and I believe, if you ask you shall receive. Doesn't that mean that if we pray hard enough for long enough that God will even heal America? No...no...no... and for sure you are ready to put this silly book in the trash, but please stay with me. I am in no way implying that prayer does not work. As a matter of fact, prayer itself is one of the seeds of discipleship that I have in my life as I will explain later. So yes, I believe in the power of prayer. However, I believe concerning this issue, more and a different approach is required. For example, when the nation of Israel was in the desert and needed water, God did not tell Moses to have the people pray hard and he would give them water. No, in fact He told Moses to *do something*. He told him to strike the rock with his rod. Moses obeyed. He *did something* in the striking of the rock and water came forth from the rock. The people had what they needed. The second time, in the wandering of the Jewish nation in the wilderness, in which they found themselves in need of water, God again had Moses *do something*! This time, God told Moses to speak to the rock and water would be provided. A different action was required. I believe that God demands action and that these actions are important to Him. As a matter of fact, Moses' disobedience of God by not doing what God told him to do caused Moses to not be able to enter the Promised Land. God could have just as easily saw that the Jewish nation needed water and answered their need. But He required action first. Many of the miracles that Jesus performed also required action. When Jesus made the blind man see, he first put spittle on his eyes and then had the man go and wash his eyes in the river. Jesus is Jesus! He could have just answered the man's need by healing him, but he required action. God could have just thought the universe into existence. Simple for him. But even God did something, He *spoke* the creation of it all. Remember the "and let there be…"? And finally, I would offer that Jesus, when looking at the world he saw, knew that it needed to know Him and accept Him personally. At that point, Jesus could have instructed the Apostles to pray for the world, and certainly He could answer that prayer. But Jesus didn't tell them to pray. He instructed the Apostles to go to the world. He required action on their part. (Matthew 28:19)

"Go therefore and make disciples of all nations, baptizing them

in the name of the Father and of the Son and of the Holy Spirit. "

I believe that is what He would tell us today, "Do something, don't just sit there and pray". We must stop waiting on others to do something to save our country, not the politicians, not the nation itself, not the people, and yes, not even God. *We* should do something. When the disciples were being tossed about during the storm, and Jesus came to them, walking on the water, Peter didn't pray, "Lord, come save us". No, Peter walked on the water. Consequently, while prayer works, one of the guiding principles is that God wants action! I would offer that no, electing good Christians to office and further that even prayer alone, is not the answer. But that action by the people of God is the answer. That action accompanied by prayer will result in a change in people and thus a change in our leaders and a change in our very country and the laws that govern it. So what is the action that we as individuals need to do? Yes, what is behind door number three...

THOUGHTS

- The 'right' politicians can't make our country great.

- Reliance on prayer alone won't make our country great.

- We the people have to do something to make our country great.

- It is not the water around you that is the problem. It is the water that gets in your boat that will sink you.

Chapter 5
Loving the Unlovable…

Hopefully, the shock of my assertion that prayer is not the answer to the healing of this country has now been satisfactorily explained, or at least the shock has worn off. So, how about another shock? What if this country doesn't need the healing? Ok…, ok…I know, now I have really flipped out. Don't I read the papers and watch the news? Our Christian values are being abandoned by this country. Same sex marriage is certified as acceptable by our court system. Abortion is approved of. Prayer is removed from the schools. Even the greeting, 'Merry Christmas' is replaced by 'Happy Holidays' by governmental bodies and corporations.

In America today, it's almost like we are called upon to apologize if we are practicing Christians. After all, doesn't America today view all Christians as a bunch of radical, non-inclusive, haters who want to force our way of life and beliefs on others?

I don't contradict any of these assertions about our country. Those are all unacceptable circumstances that exist now. However, maybe our circumstances may not need to change. Maybe, *we* need to change. We need to get to the very core of the problem, to its roots. Consider this thesis, maybe all the challenges are not Satan throwing up obstacles. Perhaps, God is giving us tests to make us see that *we* need to change, a deep change from within. Could it be that America needs a revival of our spirit and not an election? I'm not talking about changing the church we attend, or joining the choir, or even attending church more often. I'm talking about giving back some of what we've been given, grace. Perhaps, and I would forcefully offer that we, that is you and I as individuals, should begin to really and truly love the unlovable! That would be a great place to start.

In the first chapter of this book I recounted the story of my encounter with the old homeless looking man at the Wendy's restaurant. What would happen if we, all Christian individuals, started loving those unlovables? This country would be turned upside down and for the better. To take the concept farther, take a moment and look at your spouse, girlfriend, or boyfriend. While they may have faults, aren't they ever so easy to love? To offer my own example, my wife is what is I would offer as a beautiful lady. She has extraordinary beauty. She is so easy to love. Keeping that in mind, take an imaginary trip with me. We get in my car and drive from my home south until we intersect at Highway 165. We now head south on Highway 165 for half a mile and turn into the parking lot of the Kinder Rehabilitation and Retirement Center. Now we enter the front double glass doors and walk straight down the hall to room 102. We knock on the door and all we can hear is a grunt, but we slowly enter the room anyway. There in front of us, sitting up in her bed, is a woman with long gray hair. Her face surely reflects, by the deep wrinkles, the many years she has lived. A scorned look comes across her face as we enter because she is bewildered. She never has guests or visitors, only nurses and doctors. And even they go in, only as seldom as required. She is not pretty. She is not sweet. She's old. She's reflective of all the hatred she has for a world that has forgotten her. She is truly one of the world's "unlovables". Can you make a visit to this lady and just sit and listen to her? Can you simply take her hand, look her in the eyes, and tell her that God hasn't forgotten her and truly loves her? That's what I mean when I say we have to "Love the Unlovable". Yes, my wife is easy to love, but what about this old lady?

And then, I look at my children, (forgive the fact that I am so proud of my family). I have three boys and I am biased, but I would offer that they are all three so very lovable. They are good people. They say, 'yes sir' and 'no sir' and are respectful to people in general. You can see that I love them and I would offer that it is so easy to love them. However, let's take another imaginary trip. This time, let's head east to one of our larger cities in our state, New Orleans. We can park along any street. The person we are looking for can be found on almost every street in the Crescent City, or in fact on almost every street in any major city in the U.S. As we stroll down Poydras Street, we approach a young man who is sitting on a bench and is partially bent over. His hair is rather long and looks like it has never been groomed. As he looks up, when we get closer, we can see the earrings and the nose ring that he wears. His thin body sports tattoos covering his entire neck and arms. We dare not get too close to him because there must be a foul smell around him judging from the dirty clothes he wears. Truthfully, this young man who is probably no more than twenty years old, has the looks of a real drug addict. He is well qualified for the label of one of the world's unlovables! Can you go purchase a couple of sodas, sit down next to the young man, and offer him a drink? Can you look him in the eyes and ask him his story? Can you insure that your eyes don't reflect judgment nor condemnation, but rather grace? Can you just listen as long as he wants to talk without any preaching or thoughts that he probably deserves to be where he is? Can you gently touch his shoulder or hold his hand, and tell him that God loves him, has a plan for him, and that you are going to continue to pray for him as you get up and leave? That is what I mean when I say, we must love the unlovable. My boys are easy to love, but what about this young man?

Now, let's pretend it is Sunday morning. There you sit on that pew in that big white church on the corner of Tenth and Main Street. Certainly, you know the people in the church. You see them every Sunday because there is not a lot of change. As a matter of fact, they don't even like to change where they sit. Now, please look to your left, and imagine who you see. Now look to your right and imagine who is there. No matter which denomination, no matter what part of our country you are in, I would suggest that the results are the same. When you looked both left and right, you saw people who were appropriately dressed. They are all neat and proper. Certainly, they smiled at your glance. In other words, they were like us, very lovable. It is so comforting to be around those lovable people. However, we need to make one more trip. This time, let's head west for about thirty-five miles to a mid-sized town, Sulphur, Louisiana. But again, it could just as well be anywhere, USA. After exiting Interstate 10, we proceed to the Wal-Mart parking area. Yes, there are plenty of cars in Wal-Mart's parking lot. After all, this is rural America. This is where they shop. There are no Tiffany's or Sak's Fifth Avenue around here. These people shop Wal-Mart and there is nothing wrong with that. As we enter the store, there is a diverse group of people with shopping carts. Some are very much like us. Some are very different. But along Checkout Aisle #2 there stands a huge lady with a basket full of items. This lady must weigh over three hundred pounds. She has on skin tight pants that appear to be yoga pants. It appears that she's probably in her late twenties or early thirties. She certainly doesn't adhere to any hygiene standards. That's for sure. Since it is the middle of the day, it is probably safe to assume, that she has no job. We can't tell if she is married, but she has no wedding ring. However, there are four children tugging at her hips, and running circles around her. It looks like the children range in age from two to eight years old. As the woman unloads her cart, we notice all the chips, sweets, precooked meals, and soft drinks. Then we witness her prepare to pay for her items with a government food stamp card as she slaps at one of the youngsters tugging at her. Surely, we are in agreement, that she is one of the world's unlovables. Can you begin a conversation with her by asking how her day is going? Can you continue your conversation and talk to her about her life as she sees it? Can you just listen to her? Furthermore, can you tell her that you would like to pay for her basket of food? Can you look her in the eyes with true compassion in your heart? Can you give her a big heartfelt hug and tell her that you just want her to know that God loves her? That is what I mean when I say, we must love the unlovables!

The people who sit next to you in church may be lovable, but what about this lady? Can you love her? There are many, many examples of unlovables that are out there. They are not just poor and old. They come from everywhere and exist across all lines. Some are wealthy, some are young, some are handsome, and some may even be your neighbors. There are so many unlovables in this country, and therein lies the solution to our ills as a country. *We, as a people must start loving all those unlovables.* It is a one on one process. We don't have to do a lot of things, just the right one thing. To go on a trip, we don't need a lot of keys…just the one that starts the car.

I wish the solution was as simple as some would have it. But it is not one big thing we can do to change this country. Since I am a farm boy at heart, I will use a farm analogy. Suppose you have a one-hundred-acre field, and you want to transform it from being a barren field into being a lush field of watermelons. You can't just go out and plant one huge watermelon seed the size of a semi-truck in the middle of the 100 acres and magically have a watermelon field. No, what you have to do is plant thousands of small individual seeds. Then that barren field will become that lush watermelon field you want. The same is true of this country. If we want to change it, into what we aspire it to be, we must plant millions of seeds and let God do His God thing.

One of the best examples of a person who could love the unlovables was Mother Theresa. It is reported that a reporter once accompanied Mother Theresa as she ministered to the poor. As Mother Theresa bathed the open sores of the ill with her hands, the reporter gasped, "I couldn't do that for a million dollars"! Mother Theresa looked into the eyes of the reporter and tellingly stated, "Neither could I".

Yes, it's all about 'loving the unlovable'. If we want our country to change, *we* must learn to do it. The change needed is a change in *us*. The change must come from within, and it will transform us and this country. Can we?

THOUGHTS

- The real solution to our country's ills lies within each of us.

- The starting point for getting our country back on track and for our own personal growth is to 'love those unlovables'.

- There is no one big thing we need to do for this country. There are just millions of seeds to plant. Then the harvest will come for us and our country.

Chapter 6
Three Hour Challenge

The 'Three Hour Challenge' is a means for people of faith to effect change in themselves, change in others, and consequently a change in this country. The real focus of the 'Three Hour Challenge' is to 'love the unlovables'.

Hopefully, by now we realize that the unlovables are not simply the poor, the homeless, the not so handsome, the old, or the maimed. No, the unlovables can be the handsome, wealthy neighbor who lives next door. We all have struggles of some form or another. Consequently, the unlovable is all of us at one time or another. We all feel unlovable at times. When we are depressed, lonely, have lost a loved one, been betrayed, financially challenged, or have relationship issues, we feel the real sting of being unlovable. *We* are the ones that then need a seed.

All that is required for transformational change is for each Christian in this country today to give three hours to the process, not three hours per day, not three hours per week, not three hours per month, but three hours per year! That's right, if each person (that means you) will give just three hours per year to God's work, the challenge will be successful and change will be overwhelming!

Today, in America, according to most authorities,

approximately seventy percent (70%) of all people consider themselves Christians. That number was eighty-six percent (86%) in 1990. It is easy to see that the Christian army is losing the war. Furthermore, only sixty-four percent (64%) of those who consider themselves Christians attend church with some degree of regularity, which is defined as at least once per month.

So, let's do the math. There are 320,000,000 people in the U.S. today. According to the numbers cited by the majority of research analysts, that means that only 224,000,000 of that number consider themselves Christians. That leaves 96,000,000 who are not Christian. Let's say that one third of those Christians sitting next to you in church are unlovable. That means there is an additional 74,000,000 people that need seeds to be planted in them. So now our math indicates that we have 160,000,000 to plant the seeds and 160,000,000 who are in desperate need of the seeds. Consequently, if every Christian plants three seeds per year, then every person in need of those seeds will receive three encounters with grace per year. The good news is that the calculations most certainly work because when a person takes the 'Three Hour Challenge', the blessings are going to be so life changing that they will do many more than three per year. So, if every Christian, and by Christian I mean any person who has given their life to Christ, regardless of church afflation or denomination, were to love an unlovable for one hour, three different times in a single year, then every person in need of Christ in their lives (the unlovables) would experience three encounters in a single year. (I am allowing one hour for each seed to be planted. However, please understand that it could take as little as five minutes. It all depends on all the circumstances of that particular seed). Imagine the results!

Remember, I'm not talking about handing out a pamphlet, or preaching to them, or even giving them your testimony. No, *I'm talking about loving them at their place of need, in their area of need.*

In the previous chapter we talked about some of the different ways we can love the unlovables, such as a monetary gift, the giving of your time to just listen, or a gentle touch or hug. The list is unending and is only limited by your imagination. Think of all the struggles that people encounter, recognize those in need, and then plant the seed. These encounters will make a difference, especially considering that each person will receive at least three of these in a year if we Christians will accept the 'Three Hour Challenge'. The first encounter that the unlovable receives will get this person's attention. They will take note and know that something special happened. The second encounter, which will be planted by a different person, will result in the unlovable realizing that something is going on and it certainly will have the 'wow' factor for them. The third encounter, again by a different person, hopefully will result in the unlovable realizing that they want to know more and thus seek change in their own lives.

I can tell you from personal experience, that even though you as a person who accepts the 'Three Hour Challenge' may be committing to three encounters in a year, you will exceed that number many times over. The blessings will flow your way because you have chosen to honor God!

No one is exempt from accepting the 'Three Hour Challenge'. From young to old, active to home-bound, poor to wealthy, woman to man, child to adult, all are called and equipped with all that is needed. There is no preparation required to take the 'Three Hour Challenge'. It is not a task. It is an opportunity to give back some of what's been given to you, grace. You can share your experiences with others or you can keep them private between you and God. There certainly is no script, record keeping, or mandated reporting. It is a love and grace way to recapture everything that is good in us, others, and our country.

It really is just that simple, that over the next year, you simply offer grace to three different people at three different times using your own ideas by 'loving an unlovable'. It is best that each encounter occurs at their place and at their need. I have found that perhaps the best way to find an unlovable is to just let it happen. Your paths will cross at different places in different ways. There are so many struggling souls and opportunities out there that you will be amazed by how easy it is to find them. Most often, all you have to do is be willing to nonjudgmentally listen. You may keep a journal of your encounters but no official documentation is required. God will then do His part. It's okay to just test God and see if it works. In Malachi 3:10, God tells us to test him. Give grace and test God's goodness.

"Bring all the tithes into the storehouse so that there will be food enough in my Temple; if you do, I will open up the windows of heaven for you and pour out a blessing so great you won't have room enough to take it in! Try it! Let Me prove it to you!"

Truthfully, the 'Three Hour Challenge' is so easy and yet, like most journeys, the most difficult part is taking that first step. It requires you to have faith that it will work. Truth is, everyone has faith but most of us have 'little' faith. The good news though is that it doesn't take a person of great faith to take the 'Three Hour Challenge'. Only twice did Jesus encounter people of great faith. Once, in Matthew 8:5-10: *"When Jesus arrived in Capernaum, a Roman army captain came and pled with him to come to his home and heal his servant boy who was in bed paralyzed and racked with pain. 'Yes', Jesus said, 'I will come and heal him'. Then the officer said, 'Sir, I am not worthy to have you in my home; and it isn't necessary for you to come. If you will only stand here and say, 'be healed', my servant will get well. I know, because I am under the authority of my superior officers and I have authority over my soldiers, and I say to one, 'Go,' and he goes, and to another 'Come,' and he comes, and to my slave boy, 'Do this or that,' and he does it. And I know you have authority to tell his sickness to go- and it will go!' Jesus stood there amazed! Turning to the crowd he said, 'I haven't seen faith like this in all the land of Israel!'"*

The second, and only other time Jesus saw great faith was in Matthew 15: 22-28. *"A woman from Canaan who was living there came to him, pleading, 'Have mercy on me, O Lord, King David's Son! For my daughter has a demon within her, and it torments her constantly.' But Jesus gave her no reply-not even a word. Then his disciples urged him to send her away. 'Tell her to get going,' they said,' for she is bothering us with all her begging.' Then he said to the woman, 'I was sent to help the Jews- the lost sheep of Israel-not the Gentiles.' But she came and worshiped him and pled again, 'Sir, help me!' 'It doesn't seem right to take the bread from the children and throw it to the dogs,' he said. 'Yes, it is!' she replied, 'for even the puppies beneath the table are permitted to eat the crumbs that fall.' 'Woman,' Jesus told her,' your faith is large, and your request is granted.' And her daughter was healed right then."*

The point is clear. Don't worry about the amount of faith you have. Of all the people that Jesus encountered, He only found great faith twice. Many great things have been accomplished through men of 'little' faith. Certainly, we as Christians don't need to try to conjure up great faith. We don't need to try to convince God or ourselves that we have more faith than we do. We need to accept the simplicity of it. As one person said,"If we don't accept the simplicity of it, we may drown in the complexity of it." God gives us a measure of faith and always meets us at that point of faith, large or small. Many great, Spirit-led men of the past who have accomplished great things have more often than not done so with little faith. They all did however have enough faith to take that first step. That is how we use faith in the planting of seeds of grace, take the first step. It's just a matter of giving of yourself by loving the unlovable.

Three Hour Challenge
Summary

- Plant 3 seeds per year (You will do more).
- Everyone can do it.
- Best results when they don't expect it and can't repay it.
- Go to their place.
- Give what they need most.
- No judgment, just grace.
- Listen, don't preach.
- Let them know it's God, not you.
- Share your experiences with your church and friends.

Ideas to Ponder

(Keep in mind that it is YOUR challenge, so your ideas will be the best)

- Pray for guidance.

- If you belong to a church, explain to your pastor what you are doing.

- For your first seed, just let it happen. Don't seek out that person to give grace to. God will give you someone, maybe at the mall, gas station, Wal-Mart, grocery store, etc.

- For most people, I would suggest offering grace using a monetary gift recipient first. Those are the simplest. Remember to not just give money, but let them know it is God.

- Of your three seeds you plant, try for variety. Don't make them all monetary, or personal visits, or retirement home visits. Use a variety.

- Don't worry about the number of times you plant seeds. You will plant more than three, but the challenge will be met with only three.

- Make an attempt to cover the country with your seeds. Do them on vacation, when you travel for work, or just a planned trip to do some planting.

- Call a friend that lives far from you and have them plant a seed for you. You can send them the money if it is a monetary seed they choose.

- Pastors-if your church takes the 'Three Hour Challenge' consider a year end honor banquet.

- Young people can take the challenge, but parents need to set rules in order to ensure safety.

- Don't be afraid to use your imagination. God's got your back.

- Report that you are taking the challenge and your experiences on the 'Two Nickels and a Dime' Facebook Page, website www.twonickelsandadime.com, or email twonickelsandadime@aol.com

Ideas for Youth

- Tell your parents that you desire to take the challenge.

- Never go to an area without your parent's permission.

- If you belong to a church, share with your pastor that you wish to take the challenge.

- Always remember that you are to listen to people and offer grace, not judgment.

- Have a plan ahead of time of how to plant the seed. For example, if you decide that God leads you to visit a person in a retirement home, know ahead of time a couple of things that you can talk to them about. No preaching. Talk about normal things but in the end, let them know it's all about God and grace.

- Share your experiences in planting seeds with your peers.

- Report the seeds you planted to our Facebook Page, website, or email. Additionally, please let us know when you decide to take the challenge. Our prayer team will pray for you.

Game Plan

- While eating at a fast food restaurant that is not near your home, watch for an unlovable. If they don't ask, plant a seed of love. Example: Give a gift card with a personal note giving God the credit.

- While visiting a discount retailer, such as Wal-Mart or Dollar Store, that is not near your home, find an unlovable who is either inside or outside. Plant a seed of love if they don't expect it. Example: Initiate a conversation about them and their struggles. You can pay for their purchase or simply let them know that you care and will be praying for them.

- Visit the local mall. This is a good harvest area. Carry some nuts or cookies with you. Find an unlovable (this is a good place to find youth) and sit and talk to them, but mostly listen. Offering them nuts or cookies sometimes helps put them at ease. Make certain that when you leave, you let them know you're not a good person, you just serve a good God.

- Visit a hospital waiting room or emergency room. There you will find the unlovable. Offer grace and listen. When you leave, let them know you are giving them the greatest gift you have, prayer. Cancer centers are ripe with harvest. Keep in mind that the person you offer love to does not have to be poor. The wealthy need love also.

- Visit a retirement or assisted living home. Ask the information desk to tell you which resident has the fewest visitors, or who the latest arrival is. Visit that person, offering grace.

- Call a friend who lives in another town or another state. Explain to them what you are doing. Explain the 'Three Hour Challenge' to them. Send them twenty dollars and ask them to love an unlovable for you where they live. Be sure they understand that God gets the credit.

- While on vacation, challenge each family member to plant a seed at some point. Use your imagination. This is a great teaching tool for the family.

- Pastors- challenge your church members to take the 'Three Hour Challenge'. Periodically, ask for testimonies about results.

- Pastors- Challenge another church preferably in another state or another part of the country to take the 'Three Hour Challenge'. Each church can record the percentage of church members taking the challenge and completing the challenge. At the end of one year, compare percentages of completion with a reward for the winning church.

- While visiting a city, look for an unlovable in the Art or Garden District. If possible, get a couple of sodas or waters and sit with the person. Offer grace. Because of where you are, this person will very often be a younger, more affluent person. These people usually need someone to listen, no gift card needed.

- Purchase six discount crosses, whatever you can afford. As you sight-see in different places that you visit, if you find an unlovable whereby time or circumstances are limited, offer them a cross and tell them that you just wanted them to know that you love them and will be praying for a blessing for them. Be sure you keep a list so that you indeed can pray for them. Their name is not necessary.

- While I don't usually encourage group activities, I think this is a good one. Ask a person who is not of your denomination to join you on a challenge. Be imaginative. One example would be for the two of you to visit a subdivision with your mower and weed eater. Go house to house offering to mow and weed eat. Be sure to explain to the homeowner that there is absolutely no charge or obligation. Explain to them that it is simply a way to give back some of the grace that you have been given. Many will be skeptical and turn you down. Let them know that that is ok and you certainly will pray for them. This is also a planting that will work in any neighborhood, even the most affluent. Be sure to let them know that it is not a kind act, but rather a gracious God.

- If you live in a southern state, get two or three friends together and go visit any town or city in a state in the

Northeast. After all, the people in the north are all snobs who love only money and are all extremely liberal. They are very unlovable, aren't they? Plant seeds, one on one and without prejudice. You will be surprised to learn how much we are all the same. We all face struggles and have challenges to overcome.

- If you live in a northern state, get two or three friends together and visit any town or city in a state in the south. After all, people in the south are all a bunch of rednecks who swear every other word, carry their guns on their hips, and are totally conservative. They are very unlovable, aren't they? Plant seeds one on one and without prejudice. It is ok. They are people just like you.

- Take a planned trip. It can be a short one or a longer one. On the trip, make it your goal to visit places that you would like to see such as a museum, state park, etc. Undoubtedly, you will encounter some unlovables. If not, you still had a good time. Note: you also can make it a family trip. See how many unlovables your family can count. Some you may feel led to offer grace to. Children can be included since you are with them. This is a good teaching tool.

- Visit a pastor of any domination in another town and ask him if he has any acquaintances, church members, or anyone in town who is really struggling in their faith or life circumstances. Explain to him what you are doing, taking the 'Three Hour Challenge'. Go visit the person who he tells you about. Offer grace. Take to that person what that person needs most. For example, if the struggle is financial, take a gift card.

- Go to a florist and purchase several bouquets of flowers. Visit a neighborhood. Go door to door, giving the people a bouquet with a note giving credit to God. If they offer, be prepared to offer grace and listen.

- Purchase several copies of 'Two Nickels and a Dime'. Visit a neighborhood. Go door to door giving a copy to the resident. Let them know that it is an act of love because of the grace you have received in your own life.

- Pastors- This is my number one seed idea for a church to take. I even have a name for it. I call it the 'Jubilee' seed. It is only planted once every seven years. In the U.S. we are closing 3,000 churches every year. About 3,800 are started each year. From the math, we can extrapolate that we are positive net about 800 new churches per year. However, 13,024 new churches will have to be formed just to keep up with population growth for one year. Consequently, we need to start an additional 10,000 new churches each year. By the way, only six percent of the present day churches are growing. That means that ninety-four percent (94%) are losing membership. We also have six million Christians who meet weekly with a small group and never or rarely attend any church. My challenge is this. Every church should start a new church somewhere once every seven years. It will require much planning and commitment. The goal is to reach the millennials. So many tools are available. We have Facebook. We have praise and worship music. There are so many digital tools available. The church can do it alone or team with a group from another area. It is bold! There are a lot of reasons to say no to something this bold. But remember the battle is not yours...it's too big...you won't know what to do...but if your eyes are on the Lord and you have even 'little' faith, God will fight the battle.

Chapter 7
The Grace Approach

The 'Three Hour Challenge' is a grace approach to life. It is loving those unlovables! You certainly will have no trouble finding the ones in need of your seed of love. As detailed earlier, they are everywhere, in every town. The good news is that generally the encounter is not one you have to seek out. You don't have to plan to go out and complete one of your challenges or encounters. They can be every day, spur of the moment happenstances. Most of mine are just that, they just happen. What do you say to them? How do you respond to their needs? It is so easy, just show love and grace. There are no rules! We offer grace, not condemnation and guilt, and in so doing, we are not judgmental.

I recently visited with a friend who has a tremendous outreach program. He told me that he has often been involved in sessions to help churches work through certain issues. He explained to me that the issue he is involved in most often on behalf of churches is affairs between pastors and employees, usually secretaries. His point of emphasis was not that these were horrible people. They are just Christians in crisis. Guess you could say in some ways they had become one of the unlovables. Then my friend told me something that I found most profound. He said that the *Christian army is the only army in the world that crucifies it's wounded.* Wow! He was not saying that everything should be forgotten. Of course there are consequences. But what I believe my friend was saying is that those unlovables, the pastors and employees who have transgressed, were not being loved and offered grace as Jesus would want.

Seems to me the focus should be on grace and redemption and not just the consequences. I understand that the most difficult part of the equation may very well be the spouse of the pastor or the spouse of the employee. The pain, hurt, and betrayal would certainly be a deep wound. If, however, we can offer grace and love when we hurt the most, God honors that greatly. What we give to others, God returns likewise to us. Few can probably take that step, but for those who are able the reward will be unbelievable. For the Christians who are not directly involved however, we should not shout for crucifixion but rather offer great love for all those in great need. Too often we can offer grace and compassion to those who have been hurt, while being unable or unwilling to do so for those who are guilty of being the one who did the hurting. In Galatians 6:1, we are told to "gently" restore those who have done the hurting. *"Dear brothers, if a Christian is overcome by some sin, you who are godly should gently and humbly help him back onto the right path, remembering that next time it might be one of you who is in the wrong."* We all need to be "gently" restored at some point in our lives.

Mother Theresa once commented that we spend more time judging people than we do loving them. We should simply give grace and let God do his work. As the old saying goes…"I can't do God's part, and he won't do mine".

When I think of my mindset when I approach whom I consider unlovable, I am reminded of Jesus and the man he healed of leprosy. I have heard many sermons on this encounter and I agree that it was a great miracle of healing. Additionally, I realize that one of the most significant parts of the healing was when Jesus reached over and touched the man. That probably was the first time any human had touched that man in years. People didn't want his 'bad' to get on their 'good'. After all, he had leprosy. When Jesus touched the leper however, Jesus gave the man His 'good'. This healing did not begin with the touch. It actually began with this leper having a seed planted in him by someone, at some place. This man must have been told the story by someone or he would not have even been there. Someone may have loved this unlovable enough to tell him about Jesus. So it is that *the planting of a seed is when the miracle begins*. Think of the lady with the bleeding issue. She received her miracle when she touched the very garment Jesus wore. Yet, I believe the miracle actually began when someone, at some place, planted a seed in her. Someone had obviously told her about this man who had compassion for all and would heal all. So her miracle started when the seed was planted. The touch of the garment was important in that it showed her faith. However, the miracle was born out of the seed that was planted. It is the seeds that are planted that starts the miracle process. Nothing has changed. The miracles in people's lives today also start with a seed that is planted. We can start the miracle process. We must be the one to plant the seed. God will do His part. Each time we plant a seed, we should remind ourselves that we just started the miracle process. We honor God when we expect good to happen.

I remember a well-known minister from the past who would admonish people to "expect a miracle today". I would go beyond that and say, "*Start* a miracle today…Plant a seed." Those miracles are not only for the ones we plant seeds in, but also for the ones doing the planting. God works that way…everyone wins.

Most often, we think in terms of win-lose. We tend to make everything binary, a winner and a loser. We think in those terms in much of life. Athletic events are structured that way. Many business deals are set up in that manner. Our political system is structured as such. But with Jesus there are no losers when He enters the arena. Relationships with Him are always win-win. All relationships with people should be thought of in the same way. We should ensure that everyone is a winner. No one has to lose if Jesus is the center point of our relationships. Some of us think that everything is fine as long as we keep the Lord in our circle. However, it is not acceptable to just have Him *in* our circle. He must be in the *center* of our circle. For example, in our relationship circle of our life, if we push Jesus to the side of our circle, we will open up our relationships to struggles. We rationalize that since Jesus is still part of our life everything will be fine. After all, we still go to church, still tithe, and still sing "How Great Thou Art" loudly and with feeling. You can do those things and still not have Jesus in the *middle* of all the circles of your life. Jesus still needs to be the center of that circle. There are many circles in our lives; financial, health, relationships, etc. We just need to make sure that we don't push

Jesus to the edge and think that is acceptable. All of our circles are blessed and protected as long as everything revolves around that center mark, our Lord. That is one of the main reasons I have such great confidence that the 'Three Hour Challenge' will be transformational in people's lives.

Jesus was the absolute best at loving those unlovables! But to me, it is also very significant that the man with leprosy had even approached Jesus. What was he hearing that made him think he could approach this man from Galilee? After all, it was a violation of Jewish law and customs for a leper to even be in the midst of the public. Was he hearing that this Jesus was preaching and teaching guilt and condemnation such as he had probably heard his entire life, mostly from religion? No, I believe that this man with leprosy was hearing that Jesus was offering grace and love. It must have been a powerful message to get this unlovable out. That's why he had the courage to approach Jesus. Someone had obviously planted a seed. Can't you just visualize that leper crouching behind the rocks on the far side of the mountain where Jesus was proclaiming the 'Sermon on the Mount'? Perhaps, the leper was there because he had heard from others that this man Jesus was different. Maybe the 'Three Hour Challenge' is older than we think, and this leper had a grace encounter with someone like me or you. Perhaps, he had witnessed grace before and wondered what it was all about.

Jesus didn't condemn those in need, and didn't tell them that they deserved what they had. No, the leper had heard that this Jesus offered kindness and forgiveness. Can't you just see this leper slowly peek out from behind those rocks periodically to try to see this special man? Of course, he had to be careful. He would be in serious trouble if he was caught. But this message, this offer of grace, if it was true, would be worth the risk. So, I would say that one of the key components of the healing of this leper was that he even approached Jesus. And I would also offer that in the same way, if the unlovable that we encounter sees and hears grace and love, they too will seek out the source behind it. We are not Jesus, but He will certainly be there with us on our encounters. There is no way the Lord would leave us on our own in any way. He will give us the opportunities, the ability, and equip us with all we need. Ours is but to take the step.

When we offer grace, we need to be aware of prevailing thought among the people we visit. The struggle in presenting grace to a skeptical people has truly taken a turn since the new millennium. For thousands of years, the distinction has been clear between sin and Christianity. Satan's plan has always presented sin as something God wouldn't like … yet, 'it is so much fun', 'it is your right',' it makes you feel so good', and after all 'people just don't understand you'. In short, sin was not what God wanted. The line was clear. Satan promoted sin and God offered grace. It appears to me that the plan has changed. Satan's plan now appears to be to attempt to blur the lines. Instead of sin being a violation of God's law, Satan now is launching a "good war". It's no longer sin, that "bad" thing, against grace. According to Satan's plan, he would have people believe that sin is now not bad, but good. He is attempting to make us believe that it's "good vs grace". After all, we are told that being inclusive is what the world needs. And, that any lifestyle is fine and really "good". We are told that to exclude people just because they are transgender, homosexual, Islamic radicals, pro-abortion advocates, or any other group opposed to Christian values is wrong and close-minded. While I do agree that we must love these people and offer grace, that is not to say we should embrace their ideas and lifestyles. Surely, we should love them but don't live like them. Satan's attempt is to make these lifestyles "good" and any opposition to them as wrong. We should never apologize for our Christian values even though Satan is attempting to make us feel as though we are wrong. His attempt to make wrong as "good" will not stand up to grace. It is still and always will be grace against sin and not grace against "good". We should never feel like we are wrong when we follow the leadership of Christ.

At this point, perhaps we should draw a distinction between an act that is part of the 'Three Hour Challenge' and an act that is simply a good deed. Like most people, I occasionally attempt to perform good deeds. I believe that is an admirable quality in people. However, doing good deeds is not a self-defining quality of a person. Lots of people do and have done good deeds regularly and still are not living the Christian life 'real time'. An atheist can do good deeds.

Recently, I watched a story on a crime reporting channel. It was about a man named Rodney Denk. He said something I found intriguing. He said that he had always tried to do good his entire life. But, that deep down, he guessed maybe he just wasn't a good person. He testified that he had done or at least tried to do good. Trouble is Rodney Denk was a serial killer who had killed his first victim when she was just sixteen years old. So, you see *doing good deeds doesn't define us, whereas, planting seeds of discipleship does.* We must love them, not just do 'good' for them. Doing a good deed for those unlovables is not what most need. They need a seed. The seed is life changing. It shows God's compassion and instills within the person the very beginnings of what grace is and can do. Remember, miracles start with a seed. If we simply buy a meal for an unlovable, we supply an answer to a physical need for now. But if we plant a seed by showing God's love, we begin the miracle process of supplying spiritual and physical needs for now and eternity.

The 'Pay it Forward' venue is certainly an example of people doing good. My wife likes this idea. She goes through the drive thru line at McDonald's and pays for the order of the person in the vehicle behind her. This is truly a good deed. As a matter of fact, recently the lady at the order window at McDonald's in our hometown told her that after she started it one day, seven cars in a row followed suit and carried on the good deed. While this qualifies as a good deed, it is not 'loving the unlovable'. It is not a seed. It doesn't go far enough to meet the 'Three Hour Challenge.' To really qualify as loving the unlovable, the person receiving the love has to know, by some means, that Jesus is the reason for the act of compassion. They need to know that it is not simply a good person doing a good thing.

On the other hand, over a year ago, my wife, after volunteering for over sixteen years as a wish granter for a nonprofit organization, began a nonprofit entity that grants wishes to children with terminal or life threatening illnesses. It is named "Give A Wish". I could never do what she does.

Honestly, when you and I see people, especially children, with balding heads or tubes in their body don't we feel uncomfortable? Of course then comes the feeling of guilt for being uncomfortable around those who need us most. I believe we simply wish to avoid confrontation with the issues we can't solve. After all, these are what I would call optional issues. We have so many of our own primary issues to face that we subliminally try to avoid the optional problems and issues of life. The answer that I have found in handling my optional issues is to pray through it. God is helping me daily with this issue. The issue is not the children and their struggles. My attempts to avoid all optional issues is the problem. I now use a war technique for handling these issues. The military often uses 'preemptive' strikes to attack the enemy before the enemy can make their first move against them. I now use prayer as a preemptive attack on these thought patterns *before* they have time to form. When I attend an event for "Give A Wish" or meet a child for the first time, I pray and specifically thank God for all that I have, and the miracles He has performed. I thank Him for the work in the child's life. These preemptive prayers, on issues we prefer not to face, work. I even use them in other areas. For example, if a friend has just bought a new vehicle that I really love, I immediately thank God that He provides us all with great things in life. I thank Him for providing for my friend. I start these prayers as soon as I see the vehicle, in order to stop any negative patterns from even beginning. This keeps me from developing any thought patterns of jealously and want. Likewise, if I see a beautiful lady walking down the street, I immediately thank God for creating such beauty and grace. I also thank Him immediately for the wonderful wife He has given me. This is a preemptive attack against any unwanted thoughts I might develop. It works for me. It is not a "Lord help me" prayer. It is a praise prayer whereby I acknowledge God's goodness. I don't avoid the situation. I *conquer* it by giving God praise for what He has provided in my life. Rather than trying to ignore temptations and uncomfortable issues, I offer a "thank you" preemptive strike before the temptation has time to arise. I now face the temptations head on rather than trying to act as if they don't exist. I would like to believe that I am strong enough in my Christian faith that I can withstand temptations. I think we all would like to believe that. It is true that God does provide an escape from all temptations. I have found in my own life however that I am not perfect. If not careful, we all can fall into the cycle of sin and destruction. The cycle begins with the temptation. Then comes the issue of pride. We rationalize to ourselves that we can handle the situation. Whether it is a small issue or a larger one such as addiction, we convince ourselves that we will not be overcome by it. Then comes the sin. We give in to the temptation because of our pride. After all we rationalize that we are different and special. We could even rationalize it from the opposite perspective. We often say we are depressed and lonely and consequently the sin is secondary and even necessary. Whatever the rationalization, it is still sin. After we have sinned, then comes the guilt. We know when we have done wrong. This pattern of doing wrong is even true for the non-Christian. The cycle is the same. The guilt revolves right back to the temptation. Because of the guilt we feel, the temptation resurfaces. We tell ourselves that we have already given in once. Giving in to temptation becomes easier and easier. That is the cycle I have learned from different areas in my life.

First comes the temptation. It is followed by pride. Then comes the sin. Guilt is the next step. The cycle can be broken by grace. In my own life however to ensure that I don't fall prey to the cycle, I use preemptive prayer. I don't act like the temptation does not exist. I face it head on and thank God for His goodness. I don't turn my head and pretend that a beautiful lady does not exist. That would be pride and part of the cycle that I want to avoid. Instead, I thank God immediately for all the beauty He has created. A preemptive prayer blocks the cycle of sin from entering my life. The focus becomes on God and the prayer and not on the temptation. Preemptive prayers work in all areas of our lives. Preemptive prayers can keep us from giving in to thoughts of depression, loneliness, financial stresses, and any other temptations we might face. For example, if I drive into my driveway and my wife is gone on a trip for a couple of days, I know that I could feel lonely. Consequently, as soon as I turn into my driveway, I offer a preemptive prayer. I thank God for my family and all the good times ahead in our lives, and for all the good times we have already had together. Consequently, I am then thinking about God and His goodness towards me and my family. There is no more room for loneliness or depression. Preemptive prayer works! I now don't hide from my issues or temptations. I face them and strike them before they have a chance to enter my life. In this way, I have also become much more comfortable in dealing with my wife's precious children. My wife never sees the shaved heads or tubes. She only sees their smiles and she has taught me to do the same. Granting those wishes cost thousands of dollars each. My wife says she doesn't mind the fundraising however, because she loves the smiles on the children's faces when they receive what they wished for. So this act does qualify, not just as a good deed, but also as her meeting the 'Three Hour Challenge'. She makes sure that the family receiving the help understands that it is grace, not her. She gives them prayer and support. The "Give A Wish" written materials have scripture on them, and she makes sure that the children know that it is Jesus and not her and the organization. There are a lot of good organizations helping people in the world today. Few however, still have Jesus in the middle of the organization. Each time my wife and all of the faithful volunteers minister to a child and their family, they are planting seeds. The volunteers and all involved definitely meet the 'Three Hour Challenge'.

As you can see, one act my wife does is a good deed and the other act meets the "Three Hour Challenge". In one act she is doing a good deed, and in another act she is planting a seed. Hopefully, the same will be true of all of us. We should continue to give to the needy and assist the most vulnerable in society. We can do good deeds and still meet the 'Three Hour Challenge' in our life. There is room for a lot of goodness in this world.

When I was a young boy, there was a nationally renowned radio host who would broadcast the news and tell the listeners that after the commercial you will hear, "The rest of the story". Paul Harvey always had a 'page 2'. Sometimes, I think that we as Christians have neglected the 'rest of the story' in our dealings with the world. We can recite Roman's 3:23.

"since all have sinned and fall short of the glory of God" But what about the very next verse, the 'page 2', Romans 3:24...

"they are justified by his grace as a gift, through the redemption which is in Christ Jesus"

It seems we all know the sin verse, but perhaps not so much the grace verse.

Another 'rest of the story' is John 3:16. We all can recite it. We even see it on banners at ballgames and other public venues.

"For God so loved the world that he gave his only Son, that whoever believes in him should not perish but have eternal life."

But what about the next verse, John 3:17...

"For God sent the Son into the world, not to condemn the world, but that the world might be saved through him."

Again, we should note the 'page 2'. The 'no condemnation' but rather grace verse should be offered to the people who need it. Surely, we should do like Paul Harvey and ensure that our hearts reflect the 'rest of the story', that 'page 2' that is so important....

THOUGHTS

- Good deeds help show who we are, but seeds of discipleship that we plant define who we are.

- John 3:16 is important to us but so is the next verse John 3:17, the 'page 2'.

- We are not involved in a 'good' war. It is still sin against grace.

- Ants nod to each other as they pass each other. Even ants have some good qualities. We should love and offer grace, not just be 'good'.

- Preemptive prayer works.

Chapter 8
Where Are They Hiding...

A couple of years ago, I was sitting at a table in a restaurant on Lake Sam Rayburn in Brookeland, Texas. This place was called "The Stump". I was alone and enjoying a nice lunch. In typical southern tradition, I was eating some of the local flavor, chicken fried steak. As I was dipping my steak into the cream gravy, I noticed a young couple enter the restaurant and sit across two tables from me. They were a very handsome couple, very well dressed, and well groomed, especially for this place. After all, this was a lake area restaurant that catered to fishermen and water sports enthusiasts. I am neither fisherman nor water sports enthusiast. On the other hand, my wife loves everything about the water. Many people would say that I am 'going along to get along'. We have all heard that, when we do something that we really don't want to do but our spouse does. I choose to look at it differently though. I would say that I 'go along to grow along'. I believe that when I do things that my spouse enjoys even though I really don't, I contribute to both of us growing. I am blessed because I honor her and her wishes. She is blessed in knowing that I am willing to gladly give of myself just for her. This makes our marriage stronger and makes us both stronger in our belief in each other. It is not the easiest of things to do.

I always try to do those things she enjoys however with a smile and a degree of understanding that we both gain in my action. She does likewise. God honors that in both of us. Once I read that the actual damage that an earthquake does is not caused so much by the magnitude of the earthquake as it is the foundation of the structure. My wife and I both contribute to a strong foundation of our marriage. One way we do this is by doing things together that the other one enjoys. In this way we are building a foundation that will withstand any force or earthquake that comes our way. If a financial earthquake comes, we are ready. If an earthquake of depression appears, we are ready. If an earthquake of loss comes, the foundation is there for us to be able to withstand it together.

My apparel that day at the 'Stump' consisted of shorts and a polo shirt. So, I fit right in with the crowd. But this couple looked a little different. I couldn't quite put my finger on it, but there was just something about these two that intrigued me. Oh well, maybe it was the clothes they wore, the way they acted, the well-groomed hair, or maybe I was just bored. The couple received their food order about the time that I was finishing my lunch. I noticed that before they ate, they gave a blessing over their food. While I liked the fact that they prayed, I still felt that there was just something unique about that couple. I decided that the answer was to treat them as I would one of the encounters of the 'Three Hour Challenge'… plant a seed. I would show grace and love in some way. So, as I rose and walked to the cashier to pay my lunch tab, I decided that I would pay for the couple's meal. Then my plan was to walk over and tell them that I had bought their lunch, and that I was impressed to see them offer prayerful thanks over their lunch. I then would remind them that God loves them so much and respects what they do… That was the plan.

By the time I reached the cashier, however, I took one more glance over my shoulder at the couple and a very different thought pattern emerged. As I looked at the two, I realized that this couple was seemingly well to do financially and certainly didn't need me to pay for their lunch. I even concluded that since they gave a blessing over their food, they probably were in good shape spiritually. No, I decided they were not a good candidate for the planting of a seed. Therefore, I would wait and offer grace to a 'needier' person. Yes, that was good, sound reasoning. I felt so smart. Looking back now I wonder, did I really believe that God was limited in the number of blessings He would give? No, the limits are all man-made. All was great in the world, until I had driven about one mile. Very few times in my life have I been overcome by such guilt and conviction. My house on the lake was only a couple of miles away. I made it there in record time. I parked my truck in the driveway and God spoke to me, directly to my heart. The message was clear. God had given me an opportunity and a conviction to plant a seed with this young couple, and I had refused. At the thought of it, I wept. God had taught me one of the greatest lessons I have ever learned about planting seeds of discipleship. Even if someone appears to be well to do, or even very wealthy, they may need the grace and love you can offer. How they look on the outside should not determine whether you will plant a seed. I don't know what this couple was going through. Perhaps, they were experiencing relationship issues. Perhaps they were facing health issues. Maybe they had financial hurdles to struggle with. They could have been dealing with addictions. Dressed as they were, they very well could have just left the funeral of a loved one. Perhaps, they just really needed a kind gesture and reassurance that God was with them. Whatever their need, I let God and myself down that day by not showing love and giving grace to them. The lesson was clear. The 'Three Hour Challenge" candidates for encounters of love come in all forms, some poor, some rich, some young, and some are old. That's a lesson I will always remember! God burns some lessons on your heart! God, that day had led me to my place of blessing and given me all I needed. The rest was up to me....and I failed.

I can assure you that if you have any doubts about whether you can find these people that need seeds to be planted in them, remove the doubts. You will never have that issue. They will find you. God will always see that we get to our place of blessing if we are willing.

In 1 Kings 17:1-16, the prophet Elijah was told by God to go to a place by the brook Cherith because a drought was coming. God told Elijah that at that place, there would be a brook with water for him to drink and that ravens would bring him food. Ravens??? Ravens??? Ravens don't look like good food delivery boys to me. But then again, the couple in the 'Stump' didn't look like people in need of a blessing either. At least Elijah did as God directed and at his place of blessing, he received the total blessing, both meat and bread from the ravens. He received all he needed because he allowed God to take him to his place of blessing.

Later, God told Elijah to leave this area by the brook and go to another place of blessing. This time he was sent to meet a widow at a place called Zarephath. This widow was so poor that she had just enough flour and oil to prepare one last meal for her and her son. Then, they would die. This is the place of blessing where God sent Elijah? He was to expect blessings here, where a poor widow had nothing to feed him? But then again, I would never have imagined the blessing I would receive from an encounter with an old homeless looking man in Wendy's either. Funny how God uses the most unlikely! Elijah received his blessing. The widow not only fed Elijah, but she fed her entire family using the small amount she *thought* she had. As she was promised, *her jar of flour was not used up and her jug of oil did not run dry.* Wherever He leads you, and whoever He leads you to, will be the right place. It will be your place of blessing. It is there that we are called on to plant the seeds and receive our blessings.

"Now Elijah the Tishbite, of Tishbe in Gilead, said to Ahab,' As the Lord the God of Israel lives, before whom I stand, there shall be neither dew nor rain these years, except by my word.' And the word of the Lord came to him. ' depart from here and turn eastward, and hide yourself by the brook Cherith, that is east of the Jordan. You shall drink from the brook, and I have commanded the ravens to feed you there'. So he went and did according to the word of the Lord; he went and dwelt by the brook Cherith that is east of the Jordan. And the ravens brought him bread and meat in the morning, and bread and meat in the evening; and he drank from the brook. And after a while the brook dried up, because there was no rain in the land. Then the word of the Lord came to him, 'Arise, go to Zarephath, which belongs to Sidon, and dwell there. Behold, I have commanded a widow there to feed you.' So he arose

and went to Zarephath; and when he came to the gate of the city, behold, a widow was there gathering sticks; and he called to her and said,' Bring me a little water in a vessel, that I may drink.' And as she was going to bring it, he called to her and said, 'Bring me a morsel of bread in your hand.' And she said,' As the Lord your God lives, I have nothing baked, only a handful of meal in a jar, and a little oil in a cruse; and now, I am gathering a couple of sticks, that I may go in and prepare it for myself and my son, that we may eat it, and die'. And Elijah said to her,' Fear not; go and do as you have said; but first make me a little cake of it and bring it to me, and afterward make for yourself and your son. For thus says the Lord the God of Israel, 'The jar of meal shall not be spent, and the cruse of oil shall not fail, until the day that the Lord sends rain upon the earth.' And she went and did as Elijah said; and she and he, and her household ate for many days. The jar of meal was not spent, neither did the cruse of oil fail, according to the word of the Lord which he spoke by Elijah."

You never know where you will find those people that you should plant the seeds of discipleship in. What you do know with certainty is that they are in plentiful supply, and that God will lead you to them. Then the obvious question is, can we get to them all? I mean, they are everywhere. Sometime it is hard to understand how seeds of discipleship planted in rural Louisiana or anywhere else for that matter, can travel all the way across the country. But, if we plant them, they will do just that. Sociologist have actually proven that it will work. They even have a name for it. This phenomenon is called the "Six Degrees of Separation". It is a theory that everyone is six or fewer steps from any other person in the world so that a chain of 'friend of a friend' statements can be made to connect any two people in a maximum of six steps. Got it? So, if you plant a seed of discipleship such as 'loving the unlovable' in rural Louisiana, it can be replanted anywhere by another person in the United States without having to go through but no more than six other people. Sounds better than Fed Ex. Yes, it will work. Besides, all we need is 'little' faith, just enough to make that first encounter.

"Do not neglect to show hospitality to strangers, for thereby some have entertained angels unawares."

In Hebrews 13:2, we are told to be kind to strangers, because in so doing, we may be entertaining angels unaware. Sometimes, I just wonder about that couple at 'The Stump'… Just saying…

THOUGHTS

- Seeds of discipleship can be planted in people of all kinds, rich, poor, old, young, pretty, not so pretty.

- God leads us to our place of blessings if we will follow.

- Blessings often come from the strangest of circumstances.

- Always be prepared for angels unaware.

Chapter 9
It's A Beautiful Building
With A Large White Steeple

All across this beautiful country you will find churches that are absolutely gorgeous in appearance. Even in the poorest areas of any section of the country, there usually exist a church that highlights the area. Go to the most rural of parishes in Louisiana and you will find architectural witness of the generosity of a populous that takes immense pride in its church buildings. This is true no matter what the denomination. Think of some of our beautiful churches. There is the St. Louis Cathedral in New Orleans, the Cathedral Church of St. Peter and St. Paul in Washington, DC, the Memorial Presbyterian Church in St Augustine, Florida. This list is endless, from coast to coast. Of course, we all recognize that a church is so much more than a beautiful building. I mean, that is Christianity 101. But at some point, we have to ask ourselves if it is working with those beautiful buildings with their large white steeples. Please stay with me, Pastors…

Let's look at some hard data. The younger the person, the less likely they are to consider themselves Christians and attend those beautiful churches. Eighty-five percent (85%) of people born from 1920-1945 consider themselves Christians. Yet, when you consider people born from 1990-1996, only fifty-six percent (56%) of these people consider themselves Christians. That includes all Christians, Protestants and Catholics.

According to current studies, the U.S. has about six million fewer Christians today than it did in 2007. Is it fair to say or infer that the beautiful building with the large white steeple is to blame for this loss? Some would say that if everyone in this country would go to those beautiful buildings regularly perhaps this trend would reverse. But that's not happening.

Furthermore, the research shows that only sixty-four percent (64%) of those professing Christians attend church at least once per month. Once per month, what a standard! That is sixty-four percent (64%) of the seventy percent (70%) of the population, which equals thirty-four percent (34%) of the people in this country. That's only about one-third of the population who even attend church once per month. Consider then, of that number how many are 'real time' Christians?

So here we are. We've got the buildings. We've having the services. However, fewer people are attending, and less often. The trend continues and is escalating by the data. This is not an indictment. It's fact. Let's face it, and meet it head on.

Let me give you a real example of real people. Recently, my church held its revival. My church is a medium-sized (which is usually defined as having between one hundred and three hundred members) church but I consider our people extraordinarily dedicated and committed Christians. The same is true of our pastor. As we sat in the church during one night of the revival services, (It's called a Bible Conference now days. I'm not really sure why. My guess is to appeal to a younger generation.) I did a rough count of the people in attendance according to age groups. Certainly, I was not 100% correct. I do however, believe I was very accurate with my numbers. As I entered the numbers in my IPhone during the service (sorry Pastor), I began to realize that the attendees were very much disproportionately from the older generation. Out of the approximately one hundred and fifty in attendance, I recorded that perhaps, four of the attendees were from the 0-12 age group. I saw no one that I believed should be counted in the 13-35 age group. There were perhaps five present who should be considered in the 36-50 age group. Yet, in the over 50 age group was probably ninety-four percent (94%) of the attendees. This is not a condemnation of churches or revivals. It is however, highly indicative of the fact that more is needed.

Hopefully, the people who do attend the church are getting the things of God that they need. But the ones we are losing, the ones that can make all the difference, are those in need of one of our seeds.

I recently queried a pastor friend of mine as to why he thought we were losing people from our churches. He quickly and emphatically stated that over the years and up to this very day, people have seen the hypocrisy that exists. Too often, people go to church on Sunday, and that is the extent of their Christian life and principles. People, and especially young people, want to see principles that are exhibited all the time. *People want an example to live by, not just someone to go to church with.* Too many of our church attendees in the past, and for the present for that matter, may have invited Jesus into their lives, and that is where their Christian life has stopped. It seems that many of us invite Him into our lives, and then push Him to the side until we need Him. It appears that too often we want a miracle worker 'on call' rather than a Lord to always be with us. In other words, we often want the salvation without the relationship. That is the equivalent of inviting a guest to come into your home, but then telling them to just wait at the door until you need them. The world has seen this relationship between Jesus and church members too often.

Hypocrisies often exist because church attendance, and even other components of Christianity, have become cultural rather than spiritual. For too long, people have attended church because of a lot of reasons other than the one most needed. Some go for image. Some go because their family did. Some attend because they subliminally think it will improve their odds of avoiding hell. Some go to church simply because they think it is the thing to do. The world for years has seen this. *The world needs to see 'church' after church in our people.* A friend told me once that too many people who attend church today have had their 'Christianity inoculation'. What he was saying was that they have just enough Christianity to keep them from getting the real thing.

I recently read a New York Times article that told of an incident that took place in Jerusalem's Old City where many today believe is the tomb of Jesus. This particular Jerusalem tomb site has had shared ownership for centuries. Religious leaders have had guards posted at the site for centuries. In 2008, there was a brawl near the shrine where punches were thrown and even the pulling of one another's hair. Right there at the tomb of Jesus! Who were the undisciplined souls? Priests and Monks! The world sees this and it's easy to see how they would think less of all religions. People want more from religion than just a shrine…or a big beautiful church. We do need however to get them to turn to our churches and not run from them.

A friend of mine and his wife recently visited thirty churches in thirty weekends. He chose churches of different denominations and areas. I was curious as to whether or not they had noticed any one issue that troubled them about the thirty churches. He and his wife both concurred that the single issue that troubled them most about the thirty churches in general was the unfriendliness they often felt. Often when they attended a church, the very people who obviously regularly attended, gazed at them with quizzical expressions. After all, what were these two strangers doing at *their* church? I can hardly imagine how other outsiders are made to feel if they attend a service at one of these churches. Helps explain some of the reason we are losing ground. It is such a foreign thought to me. How could a house of worship built on love make anyone, at any time, feel unwelcomed? People will not go where they feel unwelcomed, especially a church. If a person is in church *only* because they are having marital problems, that's ok. They are the ones that should be there. They should feel welcomed. If a person is in church *only* because they are having financial struggles, that's ok. They are the ones that should be there. They should feel welcomed. If a person is in church only because they are experiencing health issues, it's ok. They are the ones that should be there. They should feel welcomed. If a person is *only* in church because they are having relationship issues, it's ok. They are the ones that should be there. They should feel welcomed. If a person is *only* in church because they are depressed or lonely, it's ok. They are the ones that should be there. They should feel welcomed. Churches should exist to serve those in need, those unlovables.

So how do we get them? It is not practical to expect in today's world to just go out and talk people into coming to church in order to get them to accept Christ as their Lord. That may work to a small degree, but so much more is needed. I know that I have shocked those reading this a couple of times prior to now. So, now I will make many mad. *You* are the reason the church is experiencing a decline in membership and affiliation. Yep…you! The problem is not poverty, politicians, drugs, pornography, or people who only come to church on Easter. It is us, the people who sit in the pews every Sunday.

An incident that made me think of this occurred when our two-year-old granddaughter, C'Lee, visited us after Christmas last year. For Christmas, we have a ceramic nativity scene displayed in our den. C'Lee came for a visit the week after Christmas. As she entered the den, she proceeded over to the spot where the nativity scene is always displayed. She then asked, "Where is baby Jesus"? I explained to her that we only leave the scene out for Christmas, and now it is back in the attic. There you are…Jesus back in the attic…

We sit in church, if we attend every Sunday for two hours, a total of 104 hours each year. There are 8,765 hours in a year. Where is our Jesus those other 8,661 hours or ninety-nine percent of the time? I can tell you what the numbers tell us. The world does not see our Lord in us. If it did, our churches would be full and it would be politically correct to be a Christian. The ills rest with us. We have to own it. We as church members seem to love to complain about the fact that many people only attend church for Easter Sunday or some other holiday or special event. Those people who attend only on Easter are not the problem. The problem is the ones who sit in the pews every Sunday. I include myself. I would offer that most regular church attendees could name several of these 'holiday' church goers. Yet, we should consider one question. What have we personally done, on a one on one basis, to visit those people and encourage them in their faith? I'm not talking about just church attendance. I am talking about offering grace and compassion. If in fact, we haven't extended more to the people we know who we occasionally see in church, the odds are very good that we have done little for the rest of the world to see our love…have we loved the unlovables? The world desperately needs to see a life of grace in us. This people needs to see a life of grace that exists outside of the church building the same as we portray inside the church. Too often in the past, people on the outside have only seen the hypocrisy of a people who act very differently on Sunday than they do the rest of the week. That does not mean we are going to hell. It means that because we are the problem, *we have the power to change everything.* We don't need a President, Congress, or Supreme Court, just me and you….

Our churches can make a difference. They simply need to transform themselves into what Jesus wants them to be. They need to be filled with people fully committed to doing the will of God, and offering true worship to the Lord. What matters is not the church but the people. They need to be filled with a people who offer love and grace. Matthew 21:12-15 tells us what happens to a church when it rights itself before God.

"*Jesus went into the Temple, drove out the merchants, and knocked over the money-changers' tables and the stalls of those selling doves. 'The Scriptures say my Temple is a place of prayer,' he declared,' but you have turned it into a den of thieves.' And now the blind and crippled came to him and he healed them there in the Temple. But when the chief priests and other Jewish leaders saw these wonderful miracles, and heard even the little children in the Temple shouting, 'God bless the Son of David,' they were disturbed and indignant and asked him,' Do you hear what the children are saying?'*"

Jesus ran the money-changers out of the church. After He did this, the sick, the lame, and the needy came into the Temple. He got rid of what should not have been there, the money-changers. Then the ones who needed to be there came. Today if we get rid of what shouldn't be in our churches such as hypocrisy, complacency, pride, jealously, and much more that keeps us from true worship and growth, perhaps the churches would be filled with the ones who most need it. Jesus showed us what to do with our churches and even what the result would be. Hey, even the children came and sang in the Temple Court after Jesus shook up the Temple. Wouldn't it be great to hear children sing in all of our churches again? We have acknowledged that the youth are not coming. Jesus has shown us that they will come, if we 'right' the church.

I remember an instance from my youth. A friend and I were witnessing to another friend who I'll call John, although that is not his real name. We were trying to get him to come to church. We explained that he could make his profession of faith before the entire congregation the very next Sunday. All he needed to do was to accept Jesus. We gave him the old hell, fire and brimstone. Finally, I asked John, "John, don't you want to go to heaven?" His response was more telling about us than it was about him. John, in that slow Texas drawl replied, "Yeah, I'd like to go to heaven… but I don't want to go through hell to get there." You see, we had good intentions, but now I realize that John needed a different approach. He needed a grace approach. I'm not sure if John ever accepted Jesus as his Lord, but I have prayed for him and my shortcomings.

Not long ago, I was attending a revival and the preacher had for his topic 'Righteousness'. His text was the book of Romans. I was impressed with his preaching for the first two nights. This man was a retired minister who was very sincere in what he believed. And then, on the third night, right in the middle of a sermon on his continuing theme of 'righteousness', he began a condemnation and guilt session on this country for trying to make right into wrong, and wrong into right. He cited the Bruce Jenner sex change and how it had been featured on the front cover of 'Time' magazine. He continued expressing his outrage and condemnation of both Jenner and 'Time' Magazine. Then he aimed his wrath at President Obama who he said had called Jenner, "courageous", for what he had done. He added that if you had voted for President Obama, there was a car waiting out front to take you to… He said he wouldn't finish where it would take us to. I'm not sure exactly what he meant, but I did take it to mean he was not happy with our President.

Now, I too do not believe that we should attempt to make

'wrong' into 'right'. Nor should we call 'right' as 'wrong'. Additionally, I like other Christians, do not approve of Jenner's life decisions. Further, I would concur that no president should ever use his position to condone lifestyles that violate the fabric of Christian values. But, what about the grace? It appeared to me, that this pastor forgot the 'page 2'. There truly was an awful lot of sin in this story. He could have done so much good if he had simply said he believed both of these men to be totally unlovable. You see, I know how to handle an unlovable. You love them and show grace. You don't have to agree with what they say or do, you just have to offer grace. Grace does not mean agreement or acceptance. It just means that we should give them love that they don't deserve.

Everyone in this congregation absolutely knew that the lifestyle Bruce Jenner had chosen was both sinful and shameful according to our Christian values. So, there was no teaching moment by telling us that. We knew it. But an opportunity to plant a seed in our hearts did exist at that time. I sincerely believe that if that preacher had went further and told us that yes, Bruce Jenner's lifestyle and choices truly are sinful and horrific. But, that he would like to meet Jenner someday. And if he did meet him, he would like to put his arms around him, hug him, and tell him that both God and he loves Jenner. In my opinion, that would have been the planting of a seed in us. He would have been telling us how to handle the unlovable.

The same can be said for his tirade against President Obama. He could have just as easily told us how much he detested what the president had done by saying that Jenner was courageous. Then, he had an opportunity to plant a seed. He might have told us that President Obama, because of his support of Jenner, is downright unlovable. But, that since he knew that he could never meet him, he was going to write the President a letter, and tell him that he loves him, and that he is going to pray for him asking God to send blessings his way. That would have been a seed planted. But rather, he simply told us what we all already knew. He really should have told us how to handle this unlovable.

You see, there are no degrees of unlovable to God. We are called on to offer love to even what and whom we see as the most unlovable of unlovables. This particular preacher on that particular night, could not make that leap. It doesn't matter how unlovable they are, we are called to still offer love. By the way, I truly believe this particular preacher is a real man of God, who is on fire for the Lord. I just think he needs to take the 'Three Hour Challenge'.

Hopefully, we now see that more is needed. And the truth is that I have come to believe that the church is extremely important, but what we really must do is go to 'Matthew's house'. Jesus didn't just teach in the Synagogues. He went to the sinners.

In Matthew 9: 9-13, we learned that Jesus went to the tax collector Matthew's house.

"As Jesus passed on from there, he saw a man called Matthew sitting at the tax office; and he said to him, 'Follow me.' And he rose and followed him. And as he sat at table in the house, behold, many tax collectors and sinners came and sat down with Jesus and his disciples. And when the Pharisees saw this, they said to his disciples, 'Why does your teacher eat with tax collectors and

sinners?' But when he heard it, he said, "Those who are well have no need of a physician, but those who are sick. Go and learn what this means, 'I desire mercy, and not sacrifice.' For I came not to call the righteous, but sinners."

Jesus even ate with the sinners and tax collectors while there. Keep in mind that tax collectors in those days were despised by the Jews and their religious leaders because they were corrupt and considered sinners. As a matter of fact, they were downright unlovable. And yet, there was our Lord, sitting right in the middle of them. It doesn't say so in the Bible, but I just imagine that Jesus had a grin on his face as he taught all those sinners at Matthew's house because certainly he knew what the religious leaders were thinking. Forgive my imagination but I just imagine that Jesus might have even been thinking as He looked at these religious leaders, "You ain't seen nothing yet. Wait till you see who *doesn't* make it to Heaven."

So Jesus has given us the template. We simply have to go to Matthew's house and we will find those candidates who need the planting of a seed. I have a very dear friend who is an adjunct professor at Asbury Theological Seminary. We were talking about this very subject recently, and he told me that he now tells his students to go where the need is. He tells them that they can go even to a bar, order a lemonade, and plant seeds from there. Now, that's really in Matthew's house!

We do need to go to them and minister to them wherever they are, not handing out pamphlets as we have in the past. We now need to hand out our hearts and listen without assumptions or judgments. We must stop offering a church and start offering love and grace.

I am in no way inferring that churches are not important to us and the world. I heard once that churches are a 'cup and a plane'. If I invite you to have a cup of coffee with me, you can see how that would be almost impossible if I added the stipulation of...without the cup. That would change everything. You see, it is the cup that holds everything together and enables us to enjoy the coffee inside. The church is that cup that God uses to help hold things together and enables us to grow and enjoy the Christian life. Of course, *broken* cups don't get the job done. If I invite you to fly with me to the Bahama Islands free of charge, you can see how that would be impossible if I added the stipulation of...without the airplane. That too would change everything. You see the plane is the thing that God often uses to take us where we want to go. The church is the same. It is used by the Lord to take us where we need to go. However, if the plane is broken we don't get to where we need to go.

Churches are important in many ways but don't wait in the beautiful building with the large white steeple. Go to them...

THOUGHTS

- Church membership and attendance are declining because people have been witnessing the hypocrisy for years.

- The problems of the church don't come from the people who attend church only on holidays.

- The people who sit in the pews every Sunday can change everything.

- Our pastors must preach the gospel, even the 'page 2'.

Chapter 10
Look In Their Eyes And See Their Hearts...

At the beginning of football season, I would have a team meeting. The players would all be seated in rows next to each other. Before directing our discussion to our team rule (we only had one), our schedule, our expectations, etc., I would ask that every player look to their left. Then I would ask that each player look to their right. I would then tell them that when they looked in either direction, if they saw a white teammate, they should leave the room. The younger players would be totally confused. The older, veteran players would simply smile because they knew the deal. Of course, the young players would squirm in their seats, but they wouldn't leave. They were waiting on someone else to make the first move. After a short delay, which seemed like forever to the younger players, I would continue. I would then instruct the team, this time that when they looked in either direction, if they saw any black players they should get up and leave. Again, confusion and uneasiness on the faces of the young, first year players and grins from the veteran players. Then, I would offer the explanation. You see, I would tell them, we don't have white players or black players. We have teammates. We have brothers that we are to play side by side with. We have comrades who we will learn to laugh and yes, to cry with. We have individuals of worth that we will grow with. So, I explained, we don't have any race on our team, only real people. People that we will learn to love. People that we will be able to look in their eyes and be proud because they shared our pain and our success. They understood. In all the years I coached, I never had a racial incident.

If you look in their eyes and see their heart and let them see your heart, people will respond. There is a phenomenon that I have no explanation for, but I truly believe, that if you do look directly into someone's eyes, you can see their need. You can just tell when they are hurting. Certainly, you don't see or know the 'page two' of their life but at least you have a starting point.

It is important that when we plant seeds, especially with the unlovables that we give what they need most. If you give a McDonald's gift card to the old lady in the retirement home, that won't work. Her greatest need is a visit and someone to listen. Not only do we need to give what they need, but we need to give out of our own poverty. Remember in Mark 12:41-44, the woman who dropped only two coins in the offering basket, and yet Jesus praised her as having given more than anyone else. She gave out of her poverty.

"And he sat down opposite the treasury, and watched the multitude putting money into the treasury. Many rich people put in large sums. And a poor widow came, and put in two copper coins, which make a penny. And he called his disciples to him, and said to them,' Truly, I say unto you, this poor widow has put in more than all those who are contributing to the treasury. For they all contributed out of their abundance; but she out of her poverty has put in everything she had, her whole living."

During Biblical times, people would offer what they could afford to give to God. The largest offering was the ox. Then, there was the sheep or goats. Lastly, there was the dove or pigeon. (Although, if they had absolutely nothing, a flower was acceptable). People were expected to give out of their plenty. If they were wealthy and had oxen, they were expected to offer an ox. *I wonder today, how many of us walk through our herd of oxen to get a dove or pigeon to give.* I'm not simply talking about money and tithing. I'm talking about giving of ourselves, our time, our energy, our love, and yes even seeds. We should give our best to God. We should plant as many seeds as he gives us opportunities to do so.

You may be very rich in some areas, but extremely poor in others. For example, you may be so busy that you have little extra time. Then that is exactly your area of poverty… Give of it. If you don't have time to stop and listen to the young man on Poydras Street, then do it. That's where you're giving out of your poverty meets their poverty, which is their need for someone to listen to their story. That's the point where God takes over, and oh what blessings flow.

Poverty meets poverty at grace!

God doesn't call us to be a success or a failure. He calls us to be a blessing, to plant seeds. Then comes the harvest in the form of success. Most of us want to wait until we are a 'success' to be a blessing to others. The reverse should be true. If we want to be a success, even wealthy, healthy, and wise, we need to plant seeds. That is the path to success. We study all of the habits of the wealthy, and yet the path is so simple that we often will not accept it. We want something more complicated. We want something harder to do, something we can accomplish by our own hard work.

Sometimes I believe we think God only blesses us in religious or spiritual areas. We seem to expect that He will give us peace and even good health. Too often we omit the fact that He also gives wealth and material things. To take that idea a step farther, He not only supplies wealth, but He often does so using worldly sources. As Christians, we too often think of wealth from God coming from only in the area of religious or spiritual realms. For example, we quickly acknowledge that a television evangelist probably gets great wealth from book sales and speaking engagements. That is religion supplying wealth. We can see that. God also supplies wealth to Christians by non-religious methods. That is good. Your wealth doesn't have to come from a religious source. When the Israelites were led out of Egypt by Moses, God made the Egyptians give the Israelites gold, silver, and other precious valuables. So the Israelites were given wealth by God that came from pagans. This was wealth they did not earn and from the most pagan of sources. God uses what God wants to use to provide wealth for His people. Every day I pray for wealth, health, and wisdom in a very specific way. I tell God exactly what I want. Then I leave the details up to God about how and when He provides it. The answer to my prayers may not be in the manner that I expect. In fact, it often has come from sources and ways that I never would have guessed. Assuredly though, the harvest does come and never late. I have often wondered why we as Christians are so reluctant to specifically petition God for wealth.

Many believe that we shouldn't ask for wealth. Some even

believe that God will not answer such a request. Many believe that we should only ask God for spiritual blessings. However, I would offer that wealth, when used properly, is spiritual. I have a dear friend who found out that a lady of very limited means had need of a vehicle. Her car was broken. My friend decided to plant a seed. He phoned a new car dealership and instructed them to give the lady a new car of her choosing when she visited the dealership. The lady was then told that she needed to go to the dealership. She picked out the car of her choice. My friend paid for the car. He planted that seed with love. He knew the lady didn't expect it, and certainly would never be able to repay it. God however has repaid him many times over for that one act of grace. The lady received her blessing and my friend received his harvest and will continue to do so for eternity. So, yes it is alright to pray for material things. It is the *use* of wealth that matters most.

Everything God gives us is with someone else in mind. Our use of wealth should be to plant seeds in others. By so doing, everything that God gives us continues to multiply.

When planting monetary seeds, we should never be concerned about the amount we have to offer. The amount should be what God directs you to use. No seed is too small or too big. Christians of limited means may be tempted to think that the little that they have is not important. It is never the amount. It is the act that is important. I shared twenty dollars with the man at Wendy's and yet the blessings I received were unbelievable. The blessing came from the giving of grace and not the twenty dollars. My friend who gave the car to the lady in need, gave what he was led to give. The car was not the significant part of the story. It was the act. Whether it is twenty dollars or a new car, God honors the act of giving grace. Whatever you give will be returned to you many times over. The planting of a seed is a mighty thing! It is explosive!

At this point of your grace encounter, you must be prepared for many different responses from the person you are planting the seed in. This may be their first seed, what I call the 'encounter of the first kind'. This is the one that just gets their attention, and most likely the response from them will be a quizzical look and very limited reply. Or it may be the second, third, fourth or greater seed (encounter of the second kind, encounter of the third, etc.) that they have come face to face with. Perhaps, they have begun to have questions about what's taking place. They may even ask you about grace and accepting Jesus into their lives. At this stage, you need to be ready to respond and that's not always easy since you simply don't know what to expect. After all, these are strangers that you have never met before. But remember, let God do his work!

When thinking of not knowing what to expect, I remember a humorous event from my coaching days. It was the second round of the playoffs, and I had gone out early to the practice field to get in a little extra work with our quarterbacks. One of our assistant coaches walked by a short time later and informed me that the newspaper sports writer had called and wished to speak to me. The assistant coach said he had written the newspaper's phone number in the Rolodex on my desk. After practice, I stepped into my office to return the call to the newspaper. I scrolled through the Rolodex for the number. The name of the newspaper was the Lake Charles American Press. I carefully started with the "L". Nothing was there. I proceeded to check the "C". Still no Lake Charles American Press. I then checked under the "A". Still no luck. Lastly, I checked under the "P" with no luck. There seemed to be no number. I yelled to the assistant who was still outside that I could not find the newspaper's number in my Rolodex. He responded, "Yea, Coach, it is under the "D". "D?" "D"? I yelled back at him, "How did you get "D" out of Lake Charles American Press?" "Damned newspaper", he responded. I wasn't prepared for that. So you see, you must be prepared for responses you don't expect.

The people you are offering grace to very likely see the world from a very different angle. Additionally, the response may be different if the person you are offering grace to, or planting a seed in, is someone you know who may even be from your hometown. I personally have found that loving the unlovables works better for me if it's people that I've never seen, usually away from my normal travel area. As a matter of fact, I have two basic guidelines that I try to adhere to when loving the unlovable. First, the person must be someone who doesn't expect it. I had no reservations about giving the old man at Wendy's a gift certificate. He didn't expect it. Yet, if that same man, had been standing on the side of the street with a sign asking for money, I wouldn't have given it. I'm not saying that it's wrong to give to those people. It just doesn't fit for me. They expect to receive because of what *they* are doing, holding up a sign. It is however, extremely rare for me to pass these people without praying for them. They may expect money, but I give them prayer. Then I let God be God and do His part.

My second guideline is that the person I'm offering grace to, must not be able to repay it. The 'Three Hour Challenge' as a seed planting challenge, will not work if we simply keep it amongst our church members or friends. No, we must give it to those that we may very well never see again. The only thing we should ever expect in return is the blessings from our most-high God.

One really cool way to plant a seed, such as loving the unlovable, and ensure that it travels afar is to call a friend you have that lives the farthest from you. Explain to the friend about the 'Three Hour Challenge' that you are taking. Ask your friend to help you by planting a seed in someone for you. Tell them that you wish to plant the seed of 'loving the unlovable'. If you like, send the friend some money. Have them give it to a stranger that looks in need the next time your friend is shopping or any place of their choosing. Be sure that they know to relay to the needy person that the gift comes from God, and that God loves them.

Another idea is to dedicate one hour of your next vacation to the 'Three Hour Challenge'. Along your vacation route, inevitably, you will find that person that needs you to listen to their life story. That is one way of seed planting and getting the 'Three Hour Challenge' across the globe. Oh what a difference it will make in our country and in you! There are endless ways to execute the 'Three Hour Challenge' for all people. For example, homebound people may be forced to use only the phone and computer. Youngsters may want to include parents and friends. The point is that anyone can do it, and the only limits are imposed by you. Use your imagination and ideas...

THOUGHTS

- We should never walk through our herd of oxen to get to our offering of a pigeon.

- Poverty meets poverty at grace.

- Give to those who don't expect it and can't repay it.

Stages of Encounters With The Unlovables

- 'ENCOUNTERS OF THE FIRST KIND'- This is the first time a person receives the gift of grace by the planting of a seed from someone. The person will be skeptical. They will think like we would, 'What does this person want'? Usually, they will ask where you are from and what you are doing there. They are trying to figure out your 'angle'. If it is a monetary encounter, I usually just give them the gift and tell them that God loves them and I'm praying for them. Then I leave. If it is a listening encounter, I say something to the effect about where I am from and that I was just interested in what their story is. That usually starts the person talking and I just listen. Then, when I left, I would try to always leave with a gentle touch... just a touch...probably they've been shunned enough. Be sure to let them know that it's God's grace, not you. This encounter of the first kind will serve to *get their attention.*

- 'ENCOUNTERS OF THE SECOND KIND'- This will be the second time a person receives the planting of a seed from someone, although not the person who had planted the seed in the encounter of the first time. Their first thought will be that something is going on here. Remember, that the encounter of the first kind got their attention. Now they are thinking, *'what is this'*? They will be much more open and usually will offer more detail of their circumstances, and not worry so much about your 'angle'. Still, listen to their heart. No judgment or condemnation, not even any suggestions, unless they ask you about accepting Jesus into their life. They don't need to hear your story, ideas, or suggestions. They want you to hear theirs. When you leave them, again, do so with a gentle touch and a clear statement that you are there not because you are a good person, but because you serve a good God.

- 'ENCOUNTERS OF THE THIRD KIND'- This will be the third time a person receives the gift of grace by the planting of a seed, however, not by either person who planted the first or second seed. After two previous encounters with grace, the person will most likely be much more inquisitive and seek to know more about why these things are happening. Hopefully, they will want what they have been given on two other occasions, grace. During this encounter, be prepared to answer questions about how they can accept Jesus into their lives. Still, no judgments…just let God do his part.

- When talking to the person that you are offering grace to, you may not know if it is their first, second, or third encounter. It really doesn't matter. You are simply planting a seed and God will do his part.

Chapter 11
You Just Couldn't Tell It

Sometimes it appears as though huge armies come against us in our faith and sometimes those armies are not coming from the outside but actually are from within. Surely, we all face insecurities, doubts, and fears at some point in our life. Consequently, the first obstacle we may face in taking the 'Three Hour Challenge' may be the one we least expect. Before we begin the journey, it appears to be prudent to look in the mirror. If when you look in the mirror and see any loneliness, depression, doubts or fears, then you should do what you would do for the unlovable... offer grace to yourself. I have had to offer grace to myself many times. *I have found that my strength comes from my weakness*. When I realize how weak I am, then I am forced to rely on grace. The greatest strength of Christians is not their great faith, their great speaking ability, or their great outreach. Their greatest strength is the awareness of their weakness. It is the weakness that forces us to rely on grace. From grace, God takes over.

After looking in the mirror and acknowledging our weaknesses, we are ready to accept the challenge because the 'Three Hour Challenge' is a personal thing. It is not a challenge to a religion, a denomination, nor a church. It is a challenge that *you* accept. You don't need literature, a group of people, or training.

Having said that, it should be added that there can be a place for the church. That would be a church's 'Three Hour Challenge', but for now it's a 'you' challenge. The most significant key to success in the 'Three Hour Challenge' in reaching the world, is that the world sees grace and not religion. So what role can the church play? I recently was discussing the 'Three Hour Challenge' with a pastor friend. He was excited about a church that he said was doing something very similar to what I was offering in the 'Three Hour Challenge'. Church members would stand on a street corner and pass out hot chocolate and newspapers. They would take nothing in return. They were graciously giving to the people. My friend said that in that way, there were taking the 'Three Hour Challenge' without knowing it. I love what that church is doing. Certainly, it is a very good thing. However, it is a church thing. It is a good deed. The 'Three Hour Challenge' on the other hand, is about going 'to Matthew's House' and offering grace by the planting of a seed one on one! Of course that within itself causes fears and excuses to manifest themselves. There is safety in church numbers. As a church member and participant, I'm not as exposed and vulnerable as I am one on one. The safety I refer to is not physical but rather the emotional and spiritual. We simply need to think boldly and see the world from a different perspective. I recently heard a story about a man who was having a casual conversation with a young rapper in New Orleans. They had met outside a restaurant and started talking. The man asked the young rapper why all of his songs seemed to be about killing, fighting, and sexual encounters. The young rapper replied that that is just 'life'. That is what life is all about.

The man asked the young man to walk a couple of blocks with him. He agreed. After two blocks they came to the street corner where a large church was located. People were exiting the church since service had just ended. The man asked the young man to accompany him to the entrance to talk to some of those people. He wanted the young rapper to talk to some people who had a different perspective on life. The young rapper refused. So the man had made his point. They had traveled only two blocks. He told the young man that 'life' is not that way. It was just the way he *chooses* to see life.

Most people think of themselves as quite ordinary. This is especially true in what we do in our spiritual lives. As Christians, we do the ordinary things in our Christian life. We attend services, tithe, pray, and sing in the choir. So we reason that we are ordinary. But *God always uses the ordinary to do such extraordinary things*. A stick is ordinary. Yet, God told Moses to throw a stick to the ground, and it became a serpent. That is extraordinary. In David's time, stones were very ordinary where he lived. Yet, God had David pick up stones from a brook and David slew a giant with one by using his sling shot, which by the way was very ordinary also. Slaying a giant was definitely extraordinary. Sampson used the jawbone of a donkey…and the list goes on and on throughout the Bible about God's use of the ordinary. So we should rejoice that we *think* we are ordinary. That does not limit us. It really must make God smile to see man's reaction to his use of the ordinary. And most assuredly, I do believe that God smiles.

I'm reminded about an incident that happened when my grandson was two years old. My daughter-in-law and son are

Catholic. Jace, my grandson, is of course, being raised the same. One day, they had arranged to have lunch with their priest at a local restaurant. They arrived early. When the priest walked into the restaurant, my grandson tugged at his mother and excitedly shouted, "Mom, why is Jesus here"? I have to believe that in heaven all the angels snickered and offered a little chuckle. But with all my heart, I believe that God let out a big burst of laughter! I think it's important that we do more of that, not only making God smile, but visualizing it happening. I do believe that if you accept the 'Three Hour Challenge', that will make God smile big time!

You only need to have given your life to Christ to take the challenge. If you are a Christian, you are 'challenge ready'. Brother Bob Stamps told me once that, "Everybody in San Augustine County has been saved at one time or another…you just couldn't tell it." If you take the challenge, people will be able to tell it. It truly will help *define* who you are.

If you are a Christian, that is Christian enough to take the challenge. You don't have to be an extraordinary anything. Just a regular person, who loves his Lord, qualifies you. It's important to not make excuses and talk yourself out of it. Don't listen to yourself or the devil when you tell yourself that it won't work because not enough people will take the challenge. 'Enough people' is not needed, just *you*. Don't listen to yourself when you offer the excuse that not enough people are going to be changed to make a difference. That part is God's job, and I believe He can handle that. But the real challenge will be for you to not be complacent with your Christian lifestyle. Don't accept the rationalization that you do enough since you regularly attend church, sing in the choir, and give to the needy. That is complacency. It's not a question of what you already do. It is a question of what you are *willing* to do. We should never let what we already do be an obstacle. If ever I feel sorry for myself for all I have to do, I remind myself of Caleb from the Old Testament. Caleb had been one of the twelve spies that Moses had sent out to spy out the Promised Land. Ten of the spies returned and spread fear in the Israelites. Only two of the spies, Joshua and Caleb, encouraged entering the land even though there were obstacles to overcome. The people rebelled and thus did not follow the advice of Caleb and Joshua. Consequently, the Israelites were required to wander in the wilderness for forty years. The only two people God allowed to enter the Promised Land, who had been twenty years of age or older at the time of the rebellion, was Joshua and Caleb. Now that within itself makes Caleb a hero. But what I really like is the fact that after being in the Promised Land for a few years, Caleb told Joshua that he wanted *another mountain to conquer*. The mountain he asked for was one where the giants of the land resided. Caleb was eighty-five years old when he made the request. Think of that. Here was an eighty-five-year old man asking for another mountain to conquer, where giants lived! Really, some of us get frustrated if the pastor asks us to lead service with a prayer! If an eighty-five-year old man can ask for giants, I certainly should be willing to take on the 'Three Hour Challenge'. If we look at church as our Promised Land, we need to look for some mountains! I would offer that we all need to seek out more mountains, no matter who we are and how busy we think we are.

I would add that I think that anyone taking the 'Challenge' should tell Jesus they are accepting this endeavor. You can tell Jesus privately or do so publicly. I believe acceptance of the 'Challenge' within itself is a good testimony and certainly can be shared with the church. Just try it and see what God does…in you, in your church, and in our country. This country will be changed because its people will be changed. We will be great again!!

THOUGHTS

- Offer grace to the person you know best, *you*.

- It is only a good deed unless God gets the credit.

- God uses the ordinary to do the extraordinary.

- We should always look for more mountains even after we've reached our 'Promised Land'.

- Our awareness of our weakness is where our strength begins.

Chapter 12
Watch Those Potholes...

The 'Three Hour Challenge' is primarily based on the discipleship seed of 'loving the unlovables'. The premise is that that is the key to the solution to the problems we face both as a person and as a nation. However, are there any other seeds of discipleship? Of course there are. As we take our journey, it is imperative that we don't always take the easy road. Don't always plant the seed that is easiest for you. Plant the seed that is needed most by the person God leads you to.

Planting seeds of discipleship can become, after a while, a common place event because you will begin to do it so often without even thinking about it.

Occasionally, when I return home from a visit to the mall or another city, my wife will ask if I planted any seeds. I believe that is a cool way for her to ask how my day went. By the way, that within itself is one of the small things that makes a marriage stronger. Besides, that is a conversation topic much superior to griping about the crowds in the mall or the horrible traffic. The seeds planted within us are always put there with someone else in mind. God knows exactly who is going to *need* the seed within us. He expects us to pass them to others. When God plants the seed of 'loving the unlovable' within us, He has a very specific person or persons that He wants us to share it with. When He plants the seed of prayer within us, He again has a very specific person or persons that He wants us to share it with. No matter what seed He plants in us, He has a specific destination for that seed. *Each of our seeds has someone else's name on it.*

The planting of seeds has a reach into other areas of our life. It is not a one and done thing. The acts of love we give permeate to all areas of our life. We help others, and by doing so, we make ourselves and our family stronger Christians and simply better people. The things we plant are very often returned to us in like kind. Financial returns financial, time returns time, etc... Yet there is so much more. Seeds planted have a reach into our very identity. We become in part the seeds we plant. They spread to all areas of our life. There is no downside. Our marriage strengthens, our relationships are improved, our finances are blessed, our self-image is enhanced...The best self-help tip that could ever be offered is to plant seeds. I have read many secular self-help books, and yet I have never seen that idea proposed. Usually those books give you lists and steps for self-improvement, seven steps to this and five habits of that. The *'Three Hour Challenge' offers only one step, plant seeds.* God wrote the book on this so we are guaranteed that it works. There has never been a seed planted by a Christian that has ever produced bad fruit. They always work in us and for us. Even in the area of our health, the planting of seeds has a very positive effect. Why would God leave this area of our life out of the blessings? He wouldn't and doesn't. I would be so bold as to say that if a person wants better health, they should plant some seeds. The common thought would be that you may still become ill, maybe even gravely ill, but you would have a better attitude about how to handle the health struggle. While that is true, what I am actually saying is that you will be healthier, and less likely to even become ill! The body is not immune from blessings. I would not advise anyone to stop taking their meds. Nor would I counsel anyone to discontinue the special diet and exercise program they are on. However, a good seed planting program should be a part of anyone's health plan. God wants to bless our bodies.

Planting seeds is important in the area of finances. We often seem to understand the basic concept of giving and receiving. We understand that when we give, it is returned to us many times over. Yet, I am amazed that few business people actually put the planting of financial seeds in their business plans. A business plan that includes the planting of seeds is a plan that will be blessed. If American business people went beyond financial statements, and profit and loss statements, and included a provision for seeds to be planted, they would in fact have the best bankruptcy protection ever, God.

Seed planting is so much more than a spiritual experience. It extends to all areas of our life and simply makes us better people all the way around. Because it becomes so much of our everyday life, attention should be given to ensure that it doesn't become routine and simply a matter of going through the motions. Of course, there are many parts of our Christian life that warrant this admonishment. When we sit in church each Sunday and sing, do we really pay attention to the words of the songs? Or, have we sung it so often that we sleep walk through it, while our mind wanders to the ballgame that will be on television after church? The same can be asked about the Lord's Supper. We have heard the pastor read the text and recite the ritual for partaking so often, that we must question if we ever really assess our relationship with Christ and what Communion really means personally to us.

Not long ago, I found myself in such a moment, just going through the motions. Even the planting of seeds, if we are not careful, can become a 'going through the motion' challenge. I had gone to a local convenience store to pick up a bag of ice for our family weekend get together. I was in a rather of a rush. There were very few people in the store. I could tell from her demeanor, that the cashier was not having a good day. She was rather abrupt, and certainly there was not a smile to be found. When I paid for my ice, she told me to meet her outside because she would have to bring a key out and open the ice freezer for me to get my bag of ice. I went outside and after a very short time, she hurriedly appeared. As she opened the ice freezer lock, I told her that she looked like she was having a hard day. She responded that yes in fact she was. She stated that her boss was being very unreasonable, and that she had done nothing wrong. Realizing that she needed to get back inside to work quickly, I in a very matter of fact way told her that I would say a prayer for her. She thanked me without looking up as she was trying to lock the ice freezer. I instantly felt great conviction that I had given a real 'churchy' answer to her need. I just didn't feel right. She was in a hurry to get back to her job so the encounter ended there. Truth is, I did not handle this well at all. I had simply gone through the motions because my mind was elsewhere. There is no more important place for our mind to be than on the people we meet. What I should have done is touch the woman's arm, look her in the eyes, and told her that I was going to pray specifically for her relationship with her boss, and further more I was also going to pray for her to have peace and blessings. That would have taken little more time than the routine 'I'll pray for you'. Yet, I am convinced that the result would have been different for her and me. It is not just the words we say. The words 'I'll pray for you' are not unworthy words to say to people. There is however so much effect in the touch. I believe that even a light touch on the arm or shoulder creates a connection that sends a subliminal suggestion of compassion. The 'look in the eyes' is also an effective way of bonding quickly. Looking into a person's eyes lets you not only see their struggle, but also reaffirms your interest in them as a real person. As a coach, I always told our running backs and quarterbacks that they would go wherever their eyes looked. If they looked down to the ground, that is where they would end up, on the ground. Same is true of encounters where we have an opportunity to plant a seed. We want to go to the people's need, and that means touching their hearts. We need to look in their eyes, and that will take us to their hearts.

That day I could have made a difference had I not been so 'going through the motions' in my approach.

Something good did come out of that encounter however. It has made me do a real self-evaluation of all aspects of my life to root out the routine in the areas that it shouldn't be. Some changes were simple. For example, I became more committed to listening more carefully to what my wife had to say. Because we are around our spouses so much of the time, it is quite normal to be rather inattentive to each other at times. If we find ourselves going through the motions with the person that is the most important in the world to us, it makes me wonder how we relate with all the other people we deal with. From our boss to the man who picks up our trash, everyone deserves to at least be heard and given attention by us. I realize just how important my trash collection man is when he misses my house one week. Occasionally, I now attempt to go curbside and greet the man who collects my trash. I just want him to know that I appreciate him as a person and am thankful for what he does. After all, he is not a trash man. He is someone who may be sitting next to me in Heaven someday, singing joyful praises to the Lord. I would like to think that I treated the man the same on earth as I will in Heaven.

I realized that often my mind would simply read the words when studying the Bible. After all, I had read that chapter and verse before so I often was just going through the motions. After my self-evaluation, I started making myself read the commentary about each verse. Surprising how I thought I knew the verses and yet there was much that I didn't know. Another area of struggle that I have had to overcome, since my self-evaluation, is becoming inattentive to the pastor's sermon. (I am truly sorry Brother Don.) I sometimes found that my mind would wander because I had already heard the Biblical story the pastor was telling. I realized that was pride and that somehow I needed to not be bored with what I had heard many times before. Now when I think we are entering an area whereby I might lose my concentration, I offer a preemptive prayer. In this way the focus is maintained. I will make a personal confession about the one realization that bothered me much. I realized that my mind often wandered during my prayer time.

That thought really bothered me. This was the time I was talking directly to God, and yet my mind would occasionally at random venture elsewhere. I am now committed that while I may struggle with 'going through the motions' again, I never want that to happen during my prayer time.

We must be sure that the routine doesn't take us as captive without us even realizing it. The danger is that we start liking the routine because we are comfortable there. All of us migrate by our very nature to the visible and the comfortable. Our Christian walk requires us to very often deviate from that path of least resistance. If we only follow what is visible to us, we eliminate faith and the other dimensions of the unseen in our lives. To migrate to the comfortable also does not manifest itself into a healthy walk with the Lord. That is not to say we should not be happy and content. However, at times we are called upon to be outside of our comfort zone. The love of the comfort zone can lead to a life that causes us to just go through the motions in areas of our life that we should not. Going through the motions may be alright for mowing the grass. It is not alright to go through the motions concerning matters of the heart, such as interaction with family members, spiritual events (such as the planting of seeds), worship time, and much more. If we are not careful, we can begin to love the comfortable more than we appreciate the important things. There is a sociological phenomenon known as the 'Stockholm Syndrome'. This approach explains why people whom are kidnapped, very often actually fall in love with their captor. There are many dynamic parts to this, but that is the simple explanation. During our Christian walk, we must be careful to not have the 'Stockholm Syndrome' and fall in love with what may have captured us, our comfort zone. Of course, being comfortable is within itself not sinful. We need to ensure that our love of comfort does not lead us to go through the motions when we shouldn't.

If we look at how we are to 'love the unlovable', we must meet the people at their need. With that in mind, we should not always do what is most convenient for us. For example, let's look at three different ways we can 'love the unlovable'. We can go to them at their place and listen to them. We can give them money and an admonition. We can pray for them. If we are not careful, we can begin to rely on the prayer seed and the giving of money seed too much. The idea is to offer grace. That's not to infer that prayer or monetary gifts are not acceptable ways to plant the seeds. In fact, those may be the only appropriate avenues available. Such is the case with people who are homebound or have limited access to travel. I used the giving of money to the old man in Wendy's and have used that avenue many other times. But there should be a balance in our approach to the 'Three Hour Challenge'. Use money, use prayer, use whatever God leads you to use. There are no boundaries. Don't forget those who need someone to listen. Sit with them. Listen to them. They need the touch. Remember to look into their eyes and see their hearts. Make no mistake, I do believe in the power of prayer. It is one of my other seeds of discipleship. Prayer has played such a huge role in my own personal life.

I remember a very early experience with prayer that I now look back on and see the humor as well as the genuineness. I was probably about eight years old at the time. I had stayed over-night with a cousin of mine and another friend. We attended the Pentecostal Church the next morning since it was my cousin's regular church. In those days, when people prayed, they actually got down on their knees in front of the pew. That morning, at the appropriate time, everyone on our pew got on their knees with heads bowed. I had never prayed and didn't really know what this was all about. As I knelt with my head bowed and my eyes tightly closed, I really wondered to myself what I should do. Frankly, I was afraid. I had never talked to God and had no clue as to what I should say. People were praying all around me. Then I heard my cousin, who was knelling a few feet from me say in a soft whisper, "I've got three quarters and two nickels." On the other side of my cousin was our friend and I soon heard him say, "I have four nickels and one dime." I then figured I knew how to pray. I said,"Lord, I don't know how to pray. But I have two nickels and a dime." I didn't know that my cousin and my friend were talking to each other. I assumed they were praying. Regardless, I talked to God for my very first time. I will always believe that God blessed me at that moment and heard a young boy's sincerity. I believe that God listened to my heart not my words! I don't believe God heard a young boy tell him how much money he had, but rather, He heard a young boy seeking Him. *He heard my heart.* Needless to say, prayer has always been a big part of my life and is one of my seeds of discipleship.

When I look back at how prayer has influenced my life, I find it amazing. No matter what the need, it has been met in large part due to my prayer life. Once, as a young man, who had just taken his first coaching job, I found myself in a new town with little money. To compound the issue, I wouldn't receive my first paycheck for two months. I remember that I had one $100 bill in my billfold and didn't have a checking account. I had decided to save the hundred dollar bill for an emergency. At church on Sunday, I struggled greatly as the collection plate was passed. As it reached me, for some reason, I hurriedly reached in my billfold and dropped the hundred dollar bill in the collection plate. I remember praying, "Lord, I'm giving out of my poverty, depending on you." It was a short, quick prayer. God heard it though. After all, it's not the length of the prayer that counts. When Peter had stepped out of the boat to go meet Jesus as he walked on the water, he looked down. Peter started to sink and he said a really short prayer, "Lord, save me." It worked. Jesus heard. In gest, I would offer, that if he prayed any longer, he would have drowned. My short prayer worked also. About thirty days later, through some hard work, and what some would call very good business luck, I had a little over $10,000 in my checking account. God made things come my way. It was the favor of the Lord. You can't out give God.

In December of 2014, I had a much more serious circumstance. Yes, even more serious than having no money. You guessed it, the "C" word. I remember how weak I got when my doctor gave my wife and me the news. No person is ever ready to hear those words. As my doctor gave me the treatment options, I could think of but one thing. I really needed to pray about this. After all, cancer is something that happens to *other* people. I explained to my doctor that I needed to pray, and I would come back later with our decision of the treatment option we had chosen. Of course, I included our entire family in the decision-making process. But I knew the final decision would be God's. I prayed.

I learned that some struggles are simply too big for *us* to handle. Cancer is one of those. Had I fought this battle myself I would have lost. I would have lost the physical battle and I would have lost the mental battle. Even though cancer is a physical disease of the body, it is also a very real mental struggle. I not only had to decide on treatment options, but I had to come to terms with the mental battle. Prior to this, I had always said that if I ever had cancer, I would go to Houston to MD Anderson Cancer Center for treatment. I believed that they must be the best in the world at treating cancer simply because they do it every day with the best technology available. So my immediate thought was to go there for treatment.

However, I was really unsure about what to do. Fact is, I just couldn't think very clearly. So that's where things stood. *I had a battle that was so big that I couldn't win, and I didn't know what to do.* There is always an answer in the Word. In 2Chronicles Chapter 20, Jehoshaphat was confronted by large armies coming against Judah. He knew he could not win the battle that was coming. In verse 12 of chapter 20, Jehoshaphat says, "*O our God, wilt thou not execute judgment upon them? For we are powerless against this great multitude that is coming against us. We do not know what to do, but our eyes are upon thee.*"

Here was the king of Judah admitting that they could not defeat this enemy and even admitting that they did not know what to do. That was where I was in my battle before me. I simply needed to keep my eyes on Him. Jahaziel then prophesied in verse 15, *"And he said,' Hearken, all Judah and inhabitants of Jerusalem, and King Jehoshaphat: Thus says the Lord to you. Fear not, and be not dismayed at this great multitude; for the battle is not yours but God's."* With this in mind it was obvious to me that I didn't need a super faith to defeat cancer. I simply needed enough faith to let God fight the battle, just enough faith to give the battle to Him.

Sometimes I think we try to conjure up faith that is big enough to conquer the battle we face. We seem to tell ourselves and even God, "Lord I'm believing for this miracle and just know that it is going to happen. I know You will do it. I am claiming victory for now." It seems that we are trying to convince God that we have enough faith to make it happen. I have learned that God uses the faith we have. We don't need to convince Him.

After much prayer and waiting on God's direction, I decided to not go to Houston but to stay where I believed God was directing me to for my treatment.

I had peace and God had also given me the game plan for this fight against cancer as well as all my struggles, any area...any time...All I had to do was tell God:

"The battle is too big for me."

"I don't know what to do."

"My eyes are on You, Lord."

"Accept my 'little faith'.

"The battle is the Lord's."

God did not heal me of my cancer at that time. But I did receive the greatest peace I've ever known once I decided on a treatment option. The mental battle was being taken care of by the peace given to me. From that point on, God never let me doubt. He grew my faith, and oh what a peace I felt. God used a very good doctor and robotic surgery, but he healed me. I am now cancer free, fully recovered, and back to my old self. Prostate cancer found out how small it is compared to my God. So yes, pray. It works!

THOUGHTS

- The seeds we plant are returned to us in like kind.

- The 'Three Hour Challenge' does not have lists or steps, just one thing to do, love them.

- The snail can sleep for three years straight. We shouldn't sleep walk through our Christian life.

Chapter 13
Full Circle

Every Christian has the capacity to plant seeds of discipleship in others. Seeds of discipleship, whether they be monetary seeds, time seeds, prayer seeds, 'loving the unlovables' seeds, or any of the many seeds, are not man-made. They are spiritual and not natural. God gives us the seeds. He does use many different ways to get them to us. We may receive the seed through another person as I've done before, for example on that old dusty dirt road in San Augustine county. The seed may even be planted in you in a church service. For me, I will always believe the seed of prayer was planted in me at that old Pentecostal church in east Texas before I even knew what prayer was. They are planted in all of us by God. With that said, I would add that I believe God gives those seeds to all of us who have accepted Jesus as our Lord. Most of us have seeds that we may have never used. They are within. All they need is activation. Prayer is one way to activate our seeds. We simply need to let the Lord know that we wish to start using what He has put within us. Another way to activate our seeds is plant one in someone. When you do, the race is on! It is a circle of non-stop blessings that will come your way. Think of it like a circle: God plants a seed in us. We plant that seed in someone else. *And then God blesses us many times over for giving someone something that He gave us to start with! Is that a remarkable God?* We should plant the seed that we need most. *We will receive in the form of a blessing from God the very thing we have planted in others.* God doesn't just bless us. He makes our storehouse overflow. In this area of giving by planting seeds, it is alright to test God. If you want to see how God works with the seeds of discipleship, plant a simple monetary seed in someone. It will come back to you many times over. Plant a seed of time if you are always in a rush. God will arrange it so that you are blessed with more time than you ever dreamed of. If you have relationship issues, plant in this area by the means that God provides to you. One such example, would be to visit a person in some shelter and give of yourself. God will honor that, and your own relationships will be blessed. Whatever seeds you plant will be honored by God, and the blessings from that will be too great to imagine. If you are lonely, plant a seed in that area. God will honor that. If you are having financial struggles, plant a monetary seed. I've been there and can testify that it works big time. If depression is your struggle, that is the area you need to plant in because it's your need. Depression is very real, but so is our God. God is in the restoration and healing business. I had an associate who told me about a friend of his who was really experiencing relationship issues with his son. This man said he had done everything for his son. Yet, the son was still unruly and disrespectful. This man was a Christian and couldn't understand why things didn't get better. He had prayed for his son. He said that he had given his son everything a son could want. He had even bought him a car. He tried spending time with the son after work. Nothing worked. My associate told the father that perhaps he was planting the wrong seeds, and that he should try planting a seed out of the father's poverty. Since the father had little time in light of the fact that he worked long hours, he challenged the father to just take time off work once each month for a portion of the day, and plant that seed by doing whatever the son wanted during this time off. He would thus be giving out of his poverty and meeting a need that is present in all young people, which is to spend special time with their parent…just the two of them, heart to heart. It worked. That was the seed that both needed. It came from the father's poverty and met the son's need. They began to fish together and very soon became best friends. God can heal relationships. We just need to plant some seeds.

Hopefully, we will all remember that Christianity is so much more than just leading the lost to Christ. We don't want to just get them to accept Christ into their lives. We want them to experience 'real-time' Christianity. It's not all about avoiding hell. No, it's not about subtracting. It's about adding. It is about adding seeds of discipleship in our lives and sharing those seeds with others. Since we all have seeds within us that God has put there by one means or another, we need to cast those seeds out to others. If a tree drops its seed and it falls to the base of the tree, the seed won't reproduce. However, if those seeds are caught by the wind and carried to fertile ground, they will become a big healthy tree themselves. So it is with our seeds. They need to be given out.

Please don't believe that you don't have enough faith to take the 'Three Hour Challenge'. Everyone has faith. Most of us do only have 'little' faith. But believe this, God honors 'little' faith. Remember Peter? *Peter walked on the water and yet Jesus said Peter was a man with 'little' faith.* So you see being of 'little' faith is not a deterrent. You can even walk on water if you have even 'little' faith. Use that 'little' faith and take but one step and God will honor that step and do the rest.

God gives to each of us a measure of faith. As we use that faith given to us, it grows. It is neither Biblical nor logical to think that if God has given us 'little' faith, He would deny us our needs or requests because we don't have enough faith. *God meets us at our level of faith.* If we have 'little' faith, that is where He meets us. If we have great faith that is exactly where He meets us. Faith is like a journey. When we begin the journey, we may have 'little' faith, but God is still right there with us to begin the journey. He never tells us,"when you get to point 'A' where you have more faith, I'll meet you there." So if God is with us every mile of the journey, doesn't it make sense that whatever measure of faith we have is enough faith? I may only have enough faith to sit down and start the engine, but not enough to drive that first hundred miles of a five-hundred-mile trip. God is there though as I start that engine using my 'little' faith. After God has taken me two hundred miles, I may now have more faith. He is still there. Now He uses my increased faith. And maybe after the five-hundred-mile trip is complete, I may have even more faith. God is still there. My faith grew during this trip, and God was always there no matter what my level of faith was. He met me at my level of faith all along the trip. Perhaps next time I have a five hundred mile trip, I'll have the faith I need to go even farther. 'Little' becomes great! That is true whether going on an imaginary trip, facing cancer, battling depression, fighting financial battles, losing a loved one, being betrayed, or any other challenge you face.

We started this book journey with the replanting of a seed that had been planted in me as a young boy by Brother Bob Stamps in deep east Texas, that seed of 'loving the unlovable'. He taught me what that encompasses. Brother Bob phoned me one day while I was in the process of writing this book. He said he was thinking of me that very day as he stood in line at the local grocery store in Virginia, where he now lives. There was a very large lady in front of him. He started a conversation with her and listened to her heart. As she checked out, he paid for her basket of groceries. And he told me on the phone, "Brother, I loved that unlovable and I wept"…

The seed of loving the unlovable had now gone full circle… It had traveled from east Texas to Louisiana and now to Virginia. It had gone from Brother Bob to me, and now back to Brother Bob. Yes, full circle…

THOUGHTS

- We all have seeds of discipleship in us.

- Seeds are meant to be planted in others.

- Seeds last forever.

- Don't be surprised to see a seed returned to you that was planted by you.

- Be prepared for the quiet movements in your life. Every event is not a 'Red Sea' event, even though it is still a miracle born from a seed planted.

FINAL THOUGHT

From the quiet movements to the 'Red Sea' events in our lives, it is grace that carries us through it all. Sometimes, we are doing the normal such as raising a family, and sometimes we are facing the battle of a lifetime such as cancer. Wherever we are, there is amazingly simple guidance through approaching grace in a very special way.

For additional information and materials or to schedule the author for speaking engagements please contact him at twonickelsandadime@aol.com, 337-738-8280, on facebook at Two Nickels and A Dime, or P.O. Box 778, Kinder, Louisiana 70648.

Made in the USA
Middletown, DE
14 May 2017